MW01200209

Fire Island's
Surf Hotel

The first Fire Island Lighthouse was erected in 1826 at a site approximately 200 feet southwest of the present one. It was demolished in 1858. *A drawing by Mrs. Etta Guthy and her husband for the Fire Island Lighthouse Preservation Society.*

Fire Island's Surf Hotel

and other Hostelries on Fire Island Beaches in the Nineteenth Century

Harry W. Havemeyer

Amereon
■House■

MATTITUCK, NY

To order, contact
AMEREON HOUSE,
the publishing division of
Amereon Ltd.
Post Office Box 1200
Mattituck, New York 11952
amereon@aol.com

International Standard Book Number 0-8488-3237-X

Manufactured in the United States of America

Dedication

To my wife, Genie, with whom
I have lived for 54 years
along the Great South Bay.

Robert Cushman Murphy called Fire Island the best thing of its kind from Cape Cod to Cap May. "It's the only land left that has not been heavily trampled, destroyed and bulldozed."
Page 208

Douglas Brewster, whose family has lived in Bay Shore for several generations, said, "I think we get our character from Great South Bay and I think it's a pretty good character. I've never known a mean man who would take the time to go fishing or tinker with a boat. I mean the people around here are pretty nice."
Page 14

"The bounty of the bay is not just the pleasures of the bay—it is the bounty of our own historical past, the color and sight of the bay, the strange wonderful horizon you can get on Long Island when every farm seems to evaporate into the water beyond it and there is an infinite horizon of land and sky. And the pleasure—out of time and space—even for a few minutes in our overscheduled life, of going 'on the bay'."
Page 14

From *Long Island Discovery* by Seon Manley

TABLE OF CONTENTS

A formal photograph of Felix Dominy 1800-1868, lighthouse keeper and host from 1835 to 1844, taken circa 1849. *Courtesy of Russell X. Mayer.*

AUTHOR'S NOTE AND ACKNOWLEDGMENTS

Fire Island is a name well known today to many people who live in the northern part of the country and indeed to some who live in other parts of North America. It has been widely written about as a place with a spectacular sand beach and several small communities, each with its own distinctive lifestyle. Its lighthouse, one of the tallest in the country and visible from twenty miles away, is its symbol; it is particularly well known to mariners as the first landmark visible to ships coming from Europe to the Port of New York. Its history has been written about by Madeleine C. Johnson in her book *Fire Island 1650s–1980s*, which I highly recommend. My story focuses more on the nineteenth century and touches on the twentieth century only in the Epilogue. I look upon my book as a complement to Madeleine's.

Also, I cover a larger part of the Great South Beach. The area about which I write, the barrier beach which separates the Atlantic Ocean from the Great South Bay, is known as Fire Island only to the east of the Inlet of that name. To the west it is today called Oak Beach, Cedar Beach and Gilgo Beach, where Suffolk County ends and Nassau County begins. The mainland villages opposite this section of barrier beach are Mastic Beach on the east and Amityville on the west, all within the three townships of Brookhaven, Islip and Babylon in Suffolk County. These names were generally used in the nineteenth century as well, although there were minor variations on maps of that era, for example Great South Beach, Muncie Beach and Short Beach, all of which have now disappeared.

That bold venture, the Surf Hotel, a seaside resort on Fire Island beach built in 1856 by David S.S. Sammis, seemed to many like a hopeless speculation, and when the Civil War came five years later, it appeared to be doomed to failure. It was miles away from population centers and difficult to reach by coach and ferry. Still, it did survive. By 1870 the Surf Hotel was visited by many people, some coming from great distances. This is its story.

The primary sources of my research for this book, as they were for the other books of my *Great South Bay* trilogy, have been contemporary newspapers preserved on microfilm. Both Brooklyn and New York daily papers, as well as the Babylon weekly paper the *South Side Signal*, have been used extensively. I would also like to pay tribute to the editors of that excellent magazine the *Long Island Forum*, founded in 1938 by Paul Bailey and continued under the editorship of Carl A. Starace and Richard F. Welch. Sadly, the *Forum* ceased publication with the Spring 2004 issue. However, the body of articles written and published over sixty-six years, at first monthly and later quarterly, have provided Long Island historians with a unique resource on the varying aspects of the life of this special place. I would also like to thank my friend Carl Starace, who died in 2003, for the encouragement he gave me to keep writing Long Island history.

Special thanks should also be given to the Fire Island Lighthouse Preservation Society, to its president Tom Roberts, its first vice president Bob La Rosa, its executive director Dave Griese, and all who work with them. Their efforts to keep the light bright and blinking are very important to all who live within view of it.

Several people have helped me find what I was searching for: Matt Kaminsky for Sammis's gravestone in the Babylon Cemetery, Ruth Albin for several documents at the Babylon Historical Society, Don Anselona and Jed Meade for maps at the Oak Beach Community Center, Fran Schwan for Henry Bang's history of West Island, Ralph Howell for his account of Oak Island, and Madeleine Johnson for her descriptions of Point O'Woods and Sunken Forest, and John and Natalie Montgomery for Point O'Woods photographs. Although I do much of my own research, for this book I had a great deal of help, given freely by my friend Russell X. Mayer. Russ, who grew up in Islip, Long Island, and then lived with his family in Kismet on Fire Island, became interested in the history of the area early in his life. Although he is now a United States Attorney in Omaha, Nebraska, he has maintained his great interest in Fire Island. He has shared his knowledge with me and given me many articles, including the important diaries of Felix Dominy, which I have used to relate the story of the earliest part of the Island's development. Russ certainly deserves the title of Fire Island historian, and I am particularly grateful for his interest and support.

Finally I would like to recognize the help of Dawn Chandler who has spent many hours typing my longhand onto a computer disk and Charles Gute for his editing.

Harry W. Havemeyer
July 2005

PREFACE

Although it certainly was not recognized at the time, May 17, 1835 was to become a milestone in the history of the Great South Bay. For on that day Felix Dominy arrived at the Fire Island Lighthouse to become its second keeper. The lighthouse was less than ten years old that spring, and together with the keeper's house they were the only permanent buildings on all of the thirty-mile-long South Beach. The first keeper, a Mr. Isaacs, had left after a surprisingly long tenure in such a lonely place. When Felix, his wife Phebe and their son Nathaniel came to their new home, Phebe was pregnant with another child, a girl, who would be born two months later and given the name Jerusha. During their years as lighthouse keepers she would have three more children, Arthur, Mary and Ned, born under the flashing light.

The first Fire Island Lighthouse had been completed in 1826 and was located close to the eastern side of the Fire Island Inlet. It was an eight-sided granite structure, seventy-four feet in height with a light that flashed every ninety seconds. Ship captains could distinguish it in the daytime because there were no trees anywhere nearby. However at night or in fog and bad weather it could easily be mistaken for the Sandy Hook Lighthouse that marked the entrance of New York Harbor. Or, because it lacked adequate height, it could be missed altogether with tragic results. Captains often complained about the difficulty they had in seeing the Fire Island Light. Two tragic shipwrecks were blamed directly on its lack of height: the destruction of the bark *Mexico* in 1837 off Point Lookout, with ninety passengers lost, and the immigrant ship *New Era* in 1854 with all 300 aboard lost.

The lighthouse keeper's house to which the Dominys came was located directly east of the lighthouse tower and faced north toward the Great South Bay (the second keeper's house is to the south of the present lighthouse). It was built of Connecticut River blue split stones for the foundation and sides that were twenty inches thick, as strong as the lighthouse itself, and roofed with good three-foot cedar shingles, free of sap.* The house had a full cellar, two large rooms on the ground floor with the entrance to the house in between, and stairs up to a second floor consisting of four chambers or bedrooms. There were six dormer windows on this floor—three to the north and three to the south. There were chimneys at each end of the house with fireplaces, the west one of which had an oven in the flue.

A pantry and closets were between the lower rooms. Sometime while the Dominy family was there a wood frame addition was built to provide space for the increasing number of overnight guests.

Felix Dominy was born on February 12, 1800, in East Hampton, Long Island, the son of Nathaniel and Temperance Dominy. His grandfather, also named Nathanial (1737–1813) was a notable artisan who specialized in making fine clocks. Both his grandfather and father also made fine furniture and built a reputation for craftsmanship that was unequalled on Long Island and is so recognized today. There is also a record of Felix having worked on copper sheathing for the roof of the Montauk Lighthouse.[1] On October 26, 1826, Felix married Phebe Miller, who had also been born in East Hampton in 1807, the daughter of General Jeremiah Miller and his wife Phebe Baker Miller. They would have five children. Before moving west to Fire Island, Felix had been a major and a brigade inspector of the Suffolk County militia in East Hampton. It is likely that his resourcefulness, his friendliness and a devotion to hunting and fishing led to his political appointment as the second lighthouse keeper. So began

---

* It is thought that the stones from this house were used to build the foundation of the new keeper's house in 1858 when the new lighthouse was also built. See Fire Island Light newsletter, Fall 1990, pages 6 and 7.

a period of nine years from 1835 to 1844 when Felix was keeper of the light and gradually became an innkeeper as well. Felix and Phebe took in guests for the night, then larger parties for several nights. Their home became the first resort hostelry on the Great South Bay.

During those nine years Felix kept a diary, which survives today. He always noted the weather first, then the guests for dinner and the night, and occasionally the number of fish caught by their guests. When he went away to New York or to East Hampton for a week once or twice a year, the days were left blank. In the first year or two the numbers of guests were small, but from 1838 they increased as word spread of the excellent fishing. Most came during the summer months, June through September, and, in the beginning at least, most were from Babylon to Bellport on the bay. Many were repeat visitors. There were, however, some names identified with New York City, such as Thomas Lawrance in August 1839 and Duncan Pell, auctioneer of 87 Wall Street, also that year; Rufus King in March of 1839, Edwin Thorne in September 1841, and Mr. Wilmerding and family in June 1843 as well as Mr. Schermerhorn with Philip Hone in July 1843. Hone, the famous New York diarist and early mayor, was a frequent visitor to Long Island, particularly to Fire Place (now called Brookhaven) at the eastern end of the Great South Bay to see his old friend Sam Carman. In June of 1842 he stopped at the Lighthouse for two days before proceeding on to Fire Place. Several members of the Hone family were on Dominy's register of guests between 1840 and 1846. That was important as the Hone diaries were often quoted in New York papers. His visit to an older tavern, Snedecor's Inn on the Connetquot River in 1836, gave it favorable publicity. Other visitors were the earliest summer residents of Bay Shore: Colonel Bradish Johnson and ladies in June 1840, William Lawrance and William E. Wilmerding in June 1843, as well as George C. Taylor in September 1840. Taylor would later settle in Great River where Heckscher State Park is today. Most of the guests repeated their visits in following summers. Philip Hone was recorded in three separate years. A.G. Benson, Walter Scudder from Babylon, and William Nicoll Ludlow from Oakdale came very regularly.

Dominy notes the occasional "large party," particularly over the July 4th holiday period. "Thirty-eight came from Patchogue for dinner and stayed overnight," he wrote in 1836 (he does not say where they slept). "Mrs. Nicoll and eight for dinner in June 1840; a sloop from Jersey with a large party to dine." The entry of September 13, 1842, notes that 187 bluefish were caught before breakfast, showing why the Fire Island Lighthouse "inn" had become such an attraction and why the Great South Bay would draw visitors from far and wide, long into the future. As East Islip innkeeper Amos Stellenwerf said at a later time, "In the old times the fishing was excellent and it was hard work to accommodate the people that came down here... Gold came in to Islip in the shape of city boarders... In 1849 you could get good board here for $3.00 a week. When, some years later, I raised it to $2.00 a day there was a terrible outcry, and the people said I would drive the boarders away—but I didn't."[2]

On January 15, 1844, Felix Dominy was replaced as lighthouse keeper by Captain Eliphalet Smith. His salary of $500 per year enabled him to "live very finely indeed" it was said.[3] Apparently there was a feeling in the lighthouse service that Dominy had been devoting too much time to entertaining guests and perhaps to salvaging wrecks along the beach. The superintendent, Edward Curtis, wrote in 1843 that Dominy "entertains boarders and company at his dwelling in the Island and devotes so much of his time and care to that, and other business personal to himself, that the public charge committed to him is not faithfully exercised; his lighthouse duties are made subordinate objects of attention."[4] There is no question that both charges were true, as his diaries showed.

In addition to lighthouse keeper, he was also agent for the Board of Underwriters and was asked to examine shipwrecks along the South Beach. On March 30, 1840, he wrote to his oldest son, Nathaniel, in East Hampton:

> Yesterday a brig got on shore about a mile west; in the bar—
> from Palermo in Italy, Capt. Nicolo Haggio, bound to NY
> loaded with wine, oranges, madeira nuts, almonds, figs,

raisins, lemons, grapes, anchovies, capers, apricots, preserves, cherries, etc., etc. The men eleven in number all speak Italian and one of them speaks English rather broken but we can make out to understand him so he interprets for the whole... It has been so foggy, they have not been able to board the brig since they first left her but we are in hopes of getting on board in the morning and getting out the chronometer, sailors dunnage, and a few boxes of silks and silk velvet belonging to the Captain. They seem very clever and liberal telling us to get as many nuts, oranges and lemons, wine etc. as we want.[5]

Felix also noted in his diary on February 5, 1845, that "ship Sheffield, Capt. Gilespie went on Gilgo bar 10 miles west of FI Lighthouse on a very severe gale, high tide and snow storm with a cargo of paints, oil and grindstones, coal from Hull, England." Two days later he reported starting for Gilgo and three days after that returning in a surfboat to the Dominy house. One can only imagine what salvage was aboard his surfboat.

A guest at Dominy House in 1872 perceptively commented, "Dominy's occupation while he lived in his house is open to much conjecture and still more romance. Ostensibly he kept a summer beach resort for sportsmen, but well-founded tradition says that he was next in rank to a first-class smuggler, and the stories of his wrecking activities and dubious dealings with owners' and underwriters' agents would make a book. He had departed this life when I arrived on the scene of his exploits, and his family was keeping a hotel at Bayshore, but the old house, with its curious arrangements of cellars, garrets, etc., bore mute testimony to its former owner's thrift; the outstanding barroom was made of an entire ship's cabin, completely covered on the outside with name-boards and carved work of wrecked vessels."[6]

Felix and Phebe continued to live in part of the lighthouse keeper's quarters with their children after Captain Smith arrived on February 1, 1844, to assume his duties. A new house was started in April at a location along the bayside about two-thirds of a mile east of the lighthouse. The cellar was completed that month. In May the house was framed, masons came to build the chimney, and on May 30 his diary says, "Mov'd into new house rainy P.M." On June 20 he reports, "new cabin finished house carpenter left," and on July 4, "house full." Lastly on July 15, "Mr. Nicoll Ludlow and Mr. Lawrance and family" arrived as guests. A year later on July 4, 1845, he noted that thirty to forty came to dine. What was almost immediately called Dominy House was a success. Felix continued his diaries only through October 1846. Soon after their last child Ned was born, the family left Fire Island for the winter that year for an extended visit in East Hampton with their Dominy relatives. Ned was the fourth of their five children to be born on Fire Island. Felix was forty-six years old and Phebe was almost forty. They could look forward to an interesting future as innkeepers. It should be remembered that prospects for resorts on Fire Island and along the South Shore were greatly enhanced in 1842 when the railroad from Queens County to Greenport reached Deer Park, the point directly north of Babylon. Before that, travel was only by coach and it was a two-day journey. Without the railroad it was unlikely that resort inns or hotels would have developed beyond the small hostelries such as the Dominy's Fire Island Lighthouse home.

PART I
THE SURF HOTEL

Chapter One

BEACHES, INLETS AND STORMS

What we know today as Fire Island Beach—extending from the inlet of that same name eastward to Smith Point—is a part of a barrier beach that encompasses the entire South Shore of Long Island. In earlier times it was known as the South Beach and only later was given the name of Fire Island. It is a flexible, changing strip of sand that runs in an east-west direction, unlike most barrier beaches on the Atlantic Coast that run north and south. Thus the sands on the South Beach almost always move from east to west driven by the set of the water. Like the beach itself, the inlets that allow the ocean to pass are constantly changing.

The origin of the name Fire Island is shrouded in mystery. It is clear, however, that the name for the inlet preceded that of the beach, which had been known as the Great South Beach or just the South Beach. The name Fire Island Inlet first appeared in a land deed of Henry Smith dated September 15, 1789. Before that time it was called by several other names (see following pages). One theory as to its origin is that it came from fires that were lit by Indians fishing on the beach to signal their wish to return to the mainland. Another is that because the inlet prior to 1690 was crossed by four small islands around which ocean water flowed in and out of the bay, it became known by early Dutch mapmakers as the "four island" inlet. Since the Dutch word for four sounds like fier, fier soon became fire in English usage. Those four islands exist today and are named East, Middle, West, and Sexton Island, all of which have long since been overlapped by the westward growth of the beach. There are other variations of these theories but no definitive conclusions. Perhaps both are correct.

It is likely that the Fire Island Inlet did not exist before the seventeenth century. It was not shown on maps made by early Dutch explorers. An unnamed inlet does appear, however, on the maps of John Scott ca. 1668 and of Robert Ryder ca. 1670, in approximately the correct location for the later Fire Island Inlet. As these maps are accurate in many other details, one may assume that the inlet was opened before 1668, possibly at the time of the great hurricane of 1635. Undoubtedly it was widened greatly in the storm during the winter of 1690–91, after which it became known as "Nine Mile Gut" for its great width. It was also then known as the Huntington East Gut (so mentioned in the patent for the Manor of St. George in Mastic), and the eastern side was situated at the present site of Point O'Woods by bayman Captain Charles Suydam, Islip Town Clerk and resident of South Shore Bay.[7] Suydam argued, "Eastward of Point O'Woods the vegetation is older, more dense and more varied. As we progress westward we find it to be younger, less dense, and less varied, gradually thinning out to nothing at all as we approach the present [1942] point of the Beach. [...] It is extremely doubtful if this particular strip of sand extended in 1683 much further west than the present site of Point O'Woods." He continued to argue that all the islands west of this point up to and including Captree Island were once washed by surf of the Atlantic Ocean. We know for a fact that during the nineteenth century, Oak Island Beach, Short Beach and Captree were washed by surf.

From its nine-mile width after the 1690–91 winter storm, the Fire Island Inlet retreated to about a mile in width and the beach grew to the west until 1826, when the first Fire Island Lighthouse was built; it was located at the eastern (and more stable) side of the Inlet. With time the Inlet moved westward. By 1893 it had moved a mile west of the lighthouse and began to overlap Captree Island. It also became more narrow: down to one half mile in 1910, then to 3,000 feet (somewhat larger) in 1933. It is now located about six miles west of the lighthouse and must be regularly dredged to keep it open for navigation. It overlaps all of Oak Beach and is beginning to overlap Cedar Beach to the west.

There were many other inlets through the barrier beach over recorded history. Only those cutting through to the Great South Bay will be mentioned. In addition to the Fire Island Inlet from west to east there were: the Gilgo Inlet which existed in 1755, 1764 and 1774, was closed in 1829 and 1839, and opened again from 1848 to about 1910 when it was less than a tenth of a mile wide (it was located near Gilgo Beach today); Cedar Island Inlet, which opened during the great storm of c.1764 and closed a few years later (it was located near Cedar Island today); Oak Island Inlet, which opened in 1838, closed by 1894, and was located about two miles west of the Fire Island Inlet (it was about 1,200 feet wide); Huntington East Gut, as mentioned above; and the Old or Smith Point Inlet, which existed in the 1770s and was large enough for deep-water vessels to enter the Great South Bay (it was located opposite Bellport). Two ships foundered in the mouth of the latter, which sped its closing to a trickle by 1836. Thus, during the past 350 years there have been six distinct inlets feeding the Great South Bay. Today there is only one, kept open by dredging, to keep the bay from becoming a brackish lake.

It is harder to identify the dates of the large storms that created these inlets. The first storm recorded by early Massachusetts settlers in August 1635 was in all likelihood a hurricane, based on its arrival date early in hurricane season. Its path probably followed the typical coastal route northward and would have passed eastern Long Island, affecting the South Beach. Only Indians were living in Long Island at that time. Then the winter storm of 1690–91, mentioned above, widened Fire Island Inlet to nine miles, which should have greatly expanded and deepened the Great South Bay. The inlet must have narrowed rapidly after that event, as sand from the east would have quickly flowed into the gap. Jacob Seaman, a local resident, reported that in about 1764 a great storm broke through the beach to form the Cedar Island Gut.

In the nineteenth century, the hurricane of September 23, 1815, was considered the most destructive ever known on Long Island up to that time; traveling up the Atlantic coast, it causing widespread damage along its path. Ironically it was followed in 1816 by "the summer that never came." Frost, ice and snow were reported throughout New England from June to September, caused by the volcanic eruption of Mount Tambora in Indonesia, which, it is now known, did effect the world's climate. Other nineteenth-century storms occurred in 1821, 1841, 1846, 1869, 1879, and the blizzard of 1888. Philip Hone on March 12, 1841, noted in his diary "a great storm" that made it impossible to walk in New York City. Felix Dominy in his diary noted the "severe gale and high tide" of September 9 and 10, 1846, and again on October 13, 1846. As he did not mention damage to the lighthouse or to Dominy House, these storms may not have been as severe as others.

In the twentieth century, after Fire Island became populated with homes and communities, the hurricanes became much more damaging to lives and property, although the winds were not necessarily stronger. Although there have been several hurricanes—the most recent being Hurricane Gloria in 1985—the most damage and tragic loss of life was caused by the hurricane of September 21, 1938. A splendid account of this catastrophic event can be found in chapter nine of Madeleine C. Johnson's excellent book *Fire Island 1650s–1980s.* I will only add that the storm caused the ocean to break through Fire Island in two places: at Saltaire and Cherry Grove. They were short-lived inlets. Soon after the tide returned to normal the breaks were quickly repaired by tremendous human effort, as the remaining homes were very vulnerable until that task was complete.

The next most destructive storm was in the fall of 1962. It was not officially a Fire Island hurricane because the wind never exceeded seventy miles an hour. But that storm caused extremely high tides that lasted for three days while the northeast winds tore the dunes apart. The low-pressure center had gotten blocked off New England while Long Island continued to suffer. Johnson reported, "The 1962 storm was particularly destructive: five successive high tides in forty-eight hours cut fifty sluices through the beach, carried away a hundred homes and damaged 130 more."[8] The sluices were repaired but houses were no longer allowed to be built on top of the dunes, and older houses were moved back to safer sites.

Chapter Two
THE DOMINY HOUSE
1844–1870

In the summer of 1844 Dominy House became the earliest resort inn in the Great South Bay area. Of course there were inns that had been started before; these were often coaching stops on the mainland where room and board were provided. Some became famous for their hospitality and food. To mention a few: both the LaGrange Inn and the American House, in West Islip and Babylon respectively, opened in the decade of the 1780s, following the departure of English soldiers from Long Island. They were primarily coaching stops for those traveling to points east or west on the South Country Road (Montauk Highway—Route 27A today). La Grange Inn is still a popular restaurant. Snedecor's Tavern on the Connetquot River in Great River just north of the South Country Road was opened by Eliphalet Snedecor around 1820. The tavern was continued by his son, Obadiah, until it was taken over by the South Side Sportsmen's Club of Long Island in 1866. Snedecor's Tavern was not on the Great South Bay but was very close to it down the river. It was both a coaching stop and also a resort in that guests came to hunt and fish as well as to pass through. Thus it was not solely a destination, as the Dominy House would be twenty-five years later.

The location chosen by the Dominys for their hostelry was important to its success. It was two thirds of a mile from the Fire Island Inlet on the more stable east side (at present day Kismet). To the west was Captree Beach and then the Oak Island Inlet that had recently opened. With the ever-westward drift of sand, anything built west of the Fire Island Inlet would be in trouble very soon. Captree Beach was often flooded and to its north was only marsh. Access was also important, and the trip from Babylon by sailboat across the bay and through the Whig Inlet channel to the beach east of the lighthouse could be made in an hour with a favorable wind. Security was a factor. Being near the lighthouse, a government building, at least gave the appearance of safety on a beach where shipwrecks were common and scavenging rampant. Last, being close to the Fire Island Inlet meant that guests who came for the fishing, as almost all did in the beginning, were easily able to sail out to the ocean where the biggest bluefish were feeding, sometimes in a frenzy. Dominy House had catboats for hire and bay men to take parties out to fish.

There follows a letter from an early Fire Island tourist, dated August 16, 1855, before the Surf Hotel was built, which describes a visit to the Dominy House. It has been edited in part by the editors of the *Fire Island Light* newsletter. It is a remarkably clear and expressive description of the Dominy House, the Fire Island Lighthouse, and the area around as seen from the top of the first lighthouse.

At last, after many mishaps both by land and water, we arrived at Fire Island. The question then comes, "Well what about it? It is an immense sand bank, lying south of and parallel with Long Island, thrown up by the ocean's surf, varying from one quarter to one mile wide and some forty or fifty miles long. Between it and Long Island is the Great South Bay, some eight miles wide. The most accessible way of reaching it is by Long Island Railroad to Deer Park, from thence by stage to Babylon, passing in our way to the boat a large swamp where we found mosquitos by the million, and from thence by a sailing craft across the bay.

The only buildings on this island are a Lighthouse and dwelling connected with it, two small dwelling houses occupied by fisherman and a Public House kept by Felix Dominy. The building is without any particular form, but rather a continuation of buildings which have apparently been added from time to time in order to meet its growing necessities. It is clapboarded and bears strong evidences of having been white-washed, and with its steep roofs, rough fences and shanties or out-houses surrounding it, looks more like a forsaken, dilapidated old Dutch house built a century ago than a fashionable resort for health and enjoyment.

The house was so crowded that I had allotted me with

several others, for a temporary purpose, the garret, with a seven by nine window at the gable end, looking out upon the broad blue ocean. In this room were five beds occupied by lawyers, doctors, priests, judges and sportsmen, and yet we saw nor heard any indications of disturbance whatever. The rafters above were hung with various relics of shipwrecked vessels, compasses, sails and various ornaments.

The sides of the room had never been ornamented with those modern improvements, lath and plaster. The knotholes however, were pretty much all filled up, so that it was perfectly safe to go to bed during a storm, and without fear of being blown out.

All about the premises can be seen pieces of shipwrecked vessels, broken masts, cabins, doors to staterooms, ropes and rigging from ships of every kind.

Even the pigpen and the hen roost were made of these broken fragments. The house is kept very neat and clean. The floors are without paint and scoured with white sand, and look quite like old times before paint was in much use. The meals are prepared in the best style, and not inferior, if not superior to any hotel in New York City, but without show or ornament. The best attention is paid to the guests. The proprietor and his wife are plain, intelligent and worthy people, ever ready to do a kind act or minister to the comfort and happiness of those around them. They have resided on this barren isle for twenty years and have won, by their urbanity of manner and kindness of heart, hosts of friends. Indeed, so far as real comfort is concerned it surpasses in its rustic simplicity and rudeness all the more gorgeous hotels in the state.

We have served up every day a favorite dish called clam chowder, so much relished by the late Daniel Webster. The oysters and clams, with which the table abounds in every possible variety of style, are taken a few rods from the house.

The bathing grounds are superior to any I have ever seen. The beach at first is steep, but soon you enter upon a table bottom, where one can play in the surf, meet its foamy crest and plunge into its depths, without any fear of the fatal under-tow that draws so many along these coasts into a watery grave. The sea air is undoubtedly superior at this point to most of the water places in the United States, it being surrounded with water and a constant sea breeze.

There are no means for physical exercise, but in their place there are plenty of vessels to be had for fishing excursions, the most delightful sport imaginable. Parties are constantly out, forenoons and afternoons, and take frequently in the space of an hour or two 100 or more bluefish together with various other kinds. The bluefish is the best caught for eating, and our table is constantly supplied.

Yesterday a party went out with a stiff breeze in a small schooner and passed through the inlet into the ocean, and sailed out from three to five miles from shore, dancing on the white crested wave, our boat riding there like a thing of life, the spray dashing finely over us and wetting some of our number to the skin. We met in our short journey droves of porpoises, which rolled up their immense black forms and passed us like droves of cattle.

Yesterday we took a short stroll over to the Light House, ascended to its top, and obtained a fine view of the ocean and the surrounding scenery. The lights are fourteen in number, seven arranged on each side, with reflectors, and these by a sort of clockwork are kept revolving so that about every half minute one of these sides of burners are brought to face the ocean. They are called revolving lights.

We saw at the same time a much lesser light at the keeper's house in the person of Robert Tyler, Esq. son of Ex-President Tyler (vulgarly called "Bor"). Robert was clad in a red woolen shirt and turn down collar, and had a "begone dull care" sort of a look. His wife, a common looking woman with his hat on, hunted among the children scattered among the sand banks.

On the shore nearby lies the wreck of a French packet ship from Havre, the *Two Sisters*. The figurehead, representing two sisters, stands among the relics in the chamber before mentioned. A few miles east lies the *Elizabeth*, driven ashore not long since in a terrible storm. Mrs. Margaret Fuller, a distinguished poetess, with her husband and child perished. Further west stands in full view the packet ship Sullivan, cast up high and dry in a terrible gale last winter. Indeed the coast is strewn with wrecks, masts and pieces of vessels that have been broken by the violence of the sea. Many of them, doubtless, are parts of vessels gone to pieces, and none left to tell the sad tale of their destruction.

For every part of the house the most delightful scenery presents itself to view. From my window, looking upon the ocean, I can now see vast numbers of sails from every part of the country on the fishing banks, beating about, passing and re-passing under full sail, and presenting a most animating scene. Towards the north lies Long Island, dotted with its noble mansions and hotels, and distant villages along her coast, and the bay filled with sails of every description.

On the south stretches out all around the wide ocean, with the white breakers dashing the spray as far as the eye can reach. Ships and steamships, sloops and schooners, are coursing its deep waters, and as I now sit by my window, overlooking its vast expanse, I see all kinds of craft whitening the waters with their snowy canvass, some homeward bound and some outward bound.

How many thoughts rush into the mind as one looks out upon this vast expanse of water. How much of hope, fears, anxiety, happiness and treasure now floats on its bosom, and how much lies buried beneath its waves. It is one great common leveler of human hopes and distinctions. No proud monument dare here mark the resting place of the great, while overall, both rich and poor, the evil and the just, the thundering surf, breaking in awful harmony, chaunts a requiem over its dead.[9]

The Dominy family were the proprietors of the Dominy House for many years. They watched David Sammis build his Surf Hotel to the west, blocking their unobstructed view of the lighthouse, and later enlarging it to the huge complex of buildings it would become, completely dwarfing their small hostelry. In 1861, perhaps feeling their age, Phebe and Felix turned the management over to their twenty-year-old son, Arthur, who had been born in their lighthouse home, and returned to the main land where they built a new Dominy House on the Main Street of Bay Shore village. After the railroad came to Bay Shore in 1868, it was said to be "thronged in the summer."[10]

Felix died in 1868, but Phebe continued to run the Bay Shore hotel with great flair until her death in 1891 at age eighty-four. An Islip old timer Frank Gulden wrote, "The Dominy House, not far east of the Cortland, [another hotel on Main Street] was a favorite of coaching parties from New York. It was a pleasure to sit on the piazza on a summer afternoon watching the horses and carriages go by."[11]

Phebe Miller Dominy was a consummate hostess for almost all of her adult life. After her death she was remembered by a correspondent of the *Brooklyn Times*:

The writer remembers when the Dominy House was made in the zenith of its glory. It was before the Civil War, say forty-five years ago. Its popular proprietor then was the mother of Arthur Dominy, the present Assistant Superintendent of the U.S. Life Saving Service of the district. Mrs. Dominy was a great hostess, well known throughout every state in the Union as the most hospitable boarding housekeeper between the two great oceans. While her table was always a drawing feature in itself, her ever youthful and shining personality proved a feature to herself and a blessing to her guests. Later her son Arthur Dominy conducted the Dominy House with admirable success.[12]

Although dwarfed by the Surf Hotel, the Dominy House on Fire Island Beach benefited by the closure of the former during the 1860s. Being much smaller and more intimate, it was able to stay open much later in the season to accommodate the duck hunters who came in October and November. Arthur Dominy ran the establishment until 1869 when it was sold to Captain Stephen Conklin and his wife Caroline from Babylon; they called it Dominy's Beach House to distinguish it from the Bay Shore Hotel. The Conklins kept it going for three seasons, but found times hard particularly after the expansion of the Surf in 1870. There would be more ownership changes to come as it continued to struggle on. In July 1880, *Harper's New Monthly Magazine* wrote, "In summer the surface of the Great South Bay is dotted with many dozens of sails... Sammis's Hotel and Dominy House on Fire Island send their quota." By then it was again under new ownership.

Chapter Three
EARLY RESORTS

Although Felix and Phebe Dominy in 1836 were the first to invite paying guests to their lighthouse home for the excellent bluefishing that was found nearby, and thus started the makings of a seaside resort on Fire Island, the concept of a resort did not originate on the Great South Bay.

The first important resort in the United States was started in Saratoga Springs, New York, in the 1820s. It became known as a spa because of the mineral hot springs in that area. Located thirty-five miles north of Albany, the state capital, it could be reached by a thirty-hour trip from New York City on a steam-driven ferry and then a coach ride from Albany to the hotels. After the railroad came in 1833, that journey was shortened to three to four hours, door to door, and in that year alone 8,000 people visited Saratoga. By 1840 the number had reached 12,000 and it quickly became famous as "The Queen of Spas." Grand hotels were built, such as the United States Hotel (the most fashionable in the 1840s), the Congress Hall Hotel, and after the Civil War, the Grand Union Hotel where 1,000 people were served in its dining room by 100 waiters. After the Civil War, racetracks were added and trotting races became the popular sport of the day. A gambling casino was built somewhat later. Here the noted gambling house owner Richard Canfield presided over the tables (it was legal then), where such men as Jim Fisk and "Bet-a-million" Gates won and lost large stakes. Musical concerts and bathing in the hot mineral waters rounded out the many available activities. Saratoga was not challenged until the 1870s when Newport, Rhode Island, became a serious rival for the title of "Queen." The elements that made these two resorts such a success—easy access from New York City, great comfort with good food, and plentiful recreation—were sought after by many other owners and proprietors, but never achieved to such a great degree. However, many were successful, and their numbers increased greatly after the end of the Civil War.

On Long Island, the first successful resort was located on the South Shore's barrier beach at the town of Far Rockaway in southeast Queens County. It was a day's coach ride from New York City (only Manhattan then), which was close enough for many to escape the summer heat by coming to the seashore. A hotel, known as the Marine Pavilion, was built by a group of New York investors and would attract such notable figures as the writers Henry Wadsworth Longfellow and Washington Irving, and the artist John Trumbull. It had the formidable appearance on the outside of a Greek temple with colonnades along all sides. It was so well thought of by the Long Island historian Benjamin F. Thompson that he described the resort and its grand hotel in some detail:

> Among the more remarkable features in the geography of this town is Far Rockaway, long celebrated as a fashionable watering place, and annually visited by thousands in pursuit of pure air and the luxury of sea bathing. Here the ceaseless waves of the ocean break directly upon the shore which unites at this place with the main land. The house most frequently resorted to in former times has been removed from its foundation, and its place supplied by a more extensive establishment and one better adapted to the character of the place, its eligible location as the resort of strangers, and the unrivalled sublimity and beauty of the unbounded prospect. The corner stone of the Marine Pavilion was laid June 1, 1833, with public and appropriate ceremonies, and the structure was finished soon after. It is in all respects a convenient and magnificent edifice, standing upon the margin of the Atlantic; and has generally been kept in a style not exceeded by any hotel in the United States. The main building is two hundred and thirty feet front with wings on each side, one of which is seventy-five, and the other forty-five feet in length. The peristyles are of the Ionic order, the piazza being two hundred and thirty-five feet long by twenty wide. The sleeping apartments number one hundred and sixty; the dining room is

eighty feet long, and the drawing-room fifty. It was erected originally by an association of gentlemen of the city of New York and the cost, including the land and standing furniture, exceeded $43,000. It was sold by the proprietors in May 1836, for $30,000, to Charles A. Davis and Stephen Whitney, Esqs., of New York, and the latter gentleman is now its sole owner. The atmosphere here, even in the hottest weather, is fresh, cool, and delightful; and visitors experience new inspiration and increased vigor by repeated plunges in the ocean.[13]

The Marine Pavilion burned to the ground in 1864, but was the precursor of many seaside hotels, from Coney Island to the Hamptons, that would be built after the Civil War on the famous barrier beach.* It was one of the nation's most famous early seaside resort hotels.

In the area of the Great South Bay there were very few hostelries that predated the Civil War. They could not yet be considered resorts like the Marine Pavilion at Far Rockaway. Most were little more than coaching stops or roadhouses along the South Country Road. Snedecor's Tavern and the Dominy House have been mentioned earlier. In both cases people went there to hunt or fish. Others were Amos Stellenwerf's Lake House and the Pavilion Hotel in East Islip, and Uncle Jesse Conklin's place on Captree Island, sometimes called Castle Conklin. As the railroad had not yet come to the South Shore when they opened, guests came to these by coach from either New York, or from Deer Park or North Islip where the main branch of the Long Island Railroad reached in 1842. It was a long and arduous trip, and to reach Captree Island a sailboat journey was required as well. But as word spread of the wonderful fishing in the bay and offshore at the inlet, guests did come in the decade of the 1850s to the Lake House and the Pavilion Hotel. The hotel was described in an advertisement in 1863 as follows:

---

* The Rockaway Beach Hotel opened in 1881 near the site of the Marine Pavilion.

The Hotel is fitted up in modern style, lighted with gas and furnished in a superior manner with every convenience appertaining to a "First-Class Hotel."

It is surrounded by handsome grounds, pleasant walks and drives, and has, in connection, a large Garden, Billiard and Bowling Saloons, excellent Stable accommodations, and sailboats, under the charge of experienced boatmen, for fishing—with which the bay abounds in great variety—or sailing parties of pleasure.

It is accessible from New York City by three daily trains of cars each way from James' Slip or 34th Street by the Long Island Railroad, stopping at North Islip [the South Shore line was not completed until 1868 to Islip] where stages are in readiness to carry passengers with their baggage to the Hotel. …[T]he location is unequaled by any other in the country, while its convenience to New York renders it the most eligible for the businessmen desiring to spend much of the day in the City. The house and table will be kept in the best style, and furnished in all respects to accommodate the wishes of every guest, as well as to secure the comforts of a home.[14]

The Pavilion later became a great success. It could accommodate up to 100 guests and had a stable for fifty horses. Many of the New York families who were to build homes in Islip, East Islip, and Great River in the years to follow were first guests at the Pavilion Hotel.

Uncle Jesse's Place on Captree Island was a very different establishment than the Pavilion Hotel, much more like the Dominy House on Fire Island. Uncle Jesse, from the Babylon Conklin family, advertised his hostelry as follows:

It has every appliance for entertaining any number of transient guests, with every delicacy in the shape of fish, flesh or fowl, with all other et ceteras of a first class place. Located in the direct route to the fishing ground, the place is remarkably convenient, and few parties go outside [the Inlet] without stopping. Uncle Jesse is always in the best of spirits and his roast clams and chowders are a sure prevention against sea sickness. Stop and See.[15]

Like the Dominy House, Uncle Jesse's place was very close to the Fire Island Inlet built on a high sandy bluff on the south east side of Captree Island. On the most direct route from Babylon and Bay Shore to the Atlantic Ocean by what is known as the Whig Inlet channel, it was a convenient stopping off place for every fisherman. Its overnight guests were mostly transient. Not in any sense was it an inn or a hotel. In fact, much later, Stone's Hotel was built nearby.

It should also be mentioned that the lure of bluefishing brought the first men's club to the Great South Bay when in 1854 the members of the Olympic Club decided to locate in Bay Shore at the end of Saxton Avenue. The attraction was the same for those New York City volunteer firemen of the Olympic Club as it was for the early guests at the Dominy House, the Pavilion Hotel and the future Surf Hotel.

For the glorious bluefish, one must go to the Great South Bay, and hire a catboat; or if you want the finest sport of all, go clear outside to the open ocean. Upon charter a thirty-foot catboat with one huge sail and with a crew of a man and a boy; the former to manage the boat, the latter to comment sarcastically upon the fish you do not catch. You 'pole' down the creek to the bay through clouds of mosquitos and green-headed flies: then seven miles across the bay and through the inlet to the open sea. ...Now the gulls are close at hand. Swish! The line is jerked from your nervous fingers and runs out like mad. There's a fish on the line![16]

Chapter Four

DAVID S. S. SAMMIS
1818–1865
THE EARLY YEARS

Town of Islip historian George L. Weeks Jr. began his description of the famous Surf Hotel by saying that its founder, "David Sturges Sprague Sammis, a very skillful and liberal man, was born in the Town of Huntington, near Babylon, in the year 1818. His father was Daniel Sammis, a soldier in the War of 1812."[17] As the Town of Huntington in 1818 extended south to the Atlantic Ocean, the village of Babylon, the home of Daniel and Maria Sammis and their large family of children, was its southernmost community. Babylon was a part of Huntington Town until 1872. The fact that Daniel was a soldier in that war was somewhat unusual for a man from Long Island, as the New York area was never attacked by the British as were Washington D.C. and Baltimore. However it was threatened and did prepare its defenses by calling up its militia for duty. Daniel must have become familiar with New York City during the 1812 to 1815 period of the war.

Daniel and Maria had three sons in addition to David who was born on May 8, 1818. There were also daughters in the family. They were all schooled in Babylon village in its only schoolhouse that stood on Main Street near the site of the Presbyterian Church today. It had been started in 1805 as a private school owned by a stock company that sold shares to local residents. There were only twenty-two shareholders in the beginning. In 1819, the year following David's birth, the school was sold to the people of School District No. 21, Town of Huntington, and became a public school. In 1828, when David must have been a pupil, Henry Doxsee was engaged as the schoolmaster for the sum of $30.00 per quarter! His expenses for fuel, water pail, and books came to $2.21. Apparently he was a success, as the next year he received $12.00 per month with an extra allowance of $40.00 for board.

It is not known how long young David attended this school. His parents were poor people with many children and it is likely that he was compelled to begin work at an early age. It was said that he was a quick learner, "endowed by nature with an inquiring mind, an unbending will and unflagging industry." "His lack of much schooling did not prevent him making a success of life."[18] He worked locally for a time until 1835 when he was seventeen years old, at which time, probably encouraged by his father, he left home for New York City where he could improve his prospects. He would spend more than twenty years there.

New York in 1835 was in the midst of its first real boom. In the few years since the completion of the Erie Canal, the city had become the largest in the nation primarily due to cargo being shipped from the west by barge through the canal to the port of New York. The population was rapidly growing due to immigration from Ireland, housing was expanding northward in Manhattan, and jobs were available. If one could learn a trade, the future looked especially bright. In this prosperous environment David Sammis obtained an apprenticeship with the druggist Edward A. McLean at his pharmacy at 208 Greenwich Street. This street was one of the first in Manhattan to extend from the Battery north of Wall Street to the small village of Greenwich (Greenwich Village today) where Newgate prison had been built along the Hudson River. It was an advantageous location for a business because it was a heavily trafficked road running along the west side of Manhattan where new docks were being built in the 1830s.

After two years as an apprentice at McLean's pharmacy, Sammis decided against a career as a pharmacist-chemist and left to take a position with Mackeral and Simpson, proprietors of a prosperous stage line where he remained for several years. He was fortunate to get this position, as in the year 1837 a serious financial panic hit New York and was followed by a short depression. By 1840 however, the country and city's boom was underway again. While working for the stage line he must have heard about the great resort at Saratoga Springs that was being developed and the new Marine Pavilion at Far Rockaway on Long Island. Perhaps he might have traveled to them as part of his job. In any event, being friendly by nature, he enjoyed contact with people and was drawn to the opportunity of becoming an innkeeper. There is even some evidence that as early as 1845 he began to conceive of a resort hotel for Fire Island Beach.

In 1848 at the age of thirty Sammis opened a hotel known as the East Broadway House. It was located at the corner of East Broadway and Pike Street in the Lower Eastside section of Manhattan near the East River docks where many Irish immigrants had settled. The hotel became known as a rendezvous for politicians on the Seventh Ward who were always looking for the Irish vote in return for their patronage. The famous Tammany boss William Marcy Tweed was born and grew up in the Seventh Ward very near Sammis's hotel and was often seen there in his earlier years. The East Broadway House was a success and Sammis was getting experience as a hotel operator and making money in the process. Much later he would be referred to as "an old Seventh Warder," one who took good care of his customers or guests.

During this period he began to acquire leases on the land east of the Fire Island Lighthouse and west of Dominy House. It had been used as pasture for cattle, but the ownership of it was never entirely clear. The title would be challenged from time to time in the years to come. By 1855 he had acquired leases on 120 acres of land and made the decision to begin building. He was joined by a partner, Selah Strong of Babylon, a former lighthouse keeper from 1849 to 1853, who knew the area well but was not active in the later management of the hotel. They constructed a chowder house on the beach and were ready for business for the Fourth of July, 1856. Their Babylon acquaintance Benjamin P. Field remembered "the excellent dinner he enjoyed at the shed with some friends on that Fourth."[19]

An article written in the *Brooklyn Eagle* newspaper quoted David S.S. Sammis about the beginning of his hotel that summer:

> "James Gordon Bennett [the owner and publisher of the *New York Herald*] made this house," said Mr. Sammis. "He came down here for a few days with his family and was pleased with the place. When he came to leave I presented him with his bill receipted. He refused to accept the compliment and insisted on paying. Then he went home and wrote some articles on Fire Island, and people came here from all parts of the country and made the hotel a success at once. At that time we didn't have any South Side Railroad to bring down to the bay. We used to drive four miles to the old Long Island Railroad to bring them down, sending sometimes as many as seventeen carriages after them. Now we have a horse railroad from the depot in Babylon to the dock and a steamboat across. I wish you would publish in the Eagle the time of the trains which leave Flatbush Avenue morning and evening and connect with my boat."[20]

Mr. Sammis, who was still keeping the East Broadway Hotel in Manhattan, erected the following season a structure 100 feet long, then considered large, into which he put his idle hotel help from the city and waited developments. The *Herald* articles filled the hotel with "the best people in the country," Sammis said, "and that was the beginning of the Surf Hotel."[21]

To have been able to attract the attention of James Gordon Bennett of the *New York Herald* in 1856 was an extraordinary piece of good fortune for Sammis; the *Herald* was New York's most popular daily paper, both under Bennett's ownership and then his son's in 1872 after his death. Its circulation by 1860 was 77,000, the largest of any paper in the United States, and it sold for a penny a copy. It would always actively promote the Surf Hotel, as did other papers. Of course, Sammis advertised his hotel in all the many New York and Brooklyn papers.

The 100-foot long building that was built for the season of 1857 was said to accommodate 100 guests. The following winter an addition was built and gas lighting was installed. A drawing from one advertisement that year shows a three-story structure, built on piles dug deep into the sand (in the same manner as Fire Island houses are today), of about 200 feet in length with two cupolas on the roof. The ground floor is surrounded by a piazza or porch supported by columns. There is a bathhouse for bay swimming on the left and a covered walk from the hotel to the dock at the bay where a paddle-wheel streamer is departing filled with guests. A catboat sails in the foreground and the first Fire Island Lighthouse stands on the right edge.

For the first summer season Sammis chartered the steam yacht *Bonita* from John D. Johnson, a summer resident of Islip. *Bonita* made regularly scheduled trips from the Babylon town dock across the bay to the Surf Hotel dock, providing the first regular ferry service to Fire Island. He also arranged for a coach service to and from the Babylon dock to the Deer Park depot of the Long Island Railroad to meet trains from Long Island City and Brooklyn. This was about a five-mile coach ride from depot to dock. In 1858 *Bonita* was followed by the steamer *Wave*, operated by Sammis and Henry Southard of Babylon. Sammis's resort had begun, and ho committed himself exclusively to his dream by selling the East Broadway House in New York.

Although the *New York Herald* reported many years later that the Surf Hotel was filled from the beginning with "the best people in the country," that comment was undoubtedly an exaggeration. Given the very long journey required from New York, by ferry, rail, coach and ferry again, it was very unlikely that 100 guests would have come to fill the hotel during the summer of 1857. There were not enough people of sufficient means living along the Great South Bay at that time to be able to afford more than a night or two as they had spent at the Dominy House. More importantly, the economic and political climate was changing in the entire country.

Since the early 1840s the United States had experienced a long period of growth and prosperity. This was especially so in the greater New York area. New York's merchants and industrialists were accumulating wealth, trade with China was creating fortunes for ship owners, and railroads were just beginning to be the engines of wealth they would later become. The cycle of prosperity was not to go on forever, and in 1857 it was abruptly stopped with a financial panic and two years of depression. This naturally had its effect on resorts as well. Sammis was just unlucky to have opened the Surf Hotel that year. Furthermore, the political climate was getting increasingly tense as the country headed toward the election of Abraham Lincoln as President in 1860 and the Civil War that followed.

Every piece of evidence indicates that the Surf Hotel had a slow start on Fire Island and that David Sammis showed great courage to keep it open as long as he did. In fact, on March 12, 1860, a bankruptcy petition was approved by a Suffolk County judge. It is not known how long it was closed, but it was likely not opened again until the Civil War was over. It was during those difficult years, however, that the Surf acquired a new neighbor to replace an old friend.

At the time that the Surf was preparing to open for its first season, the Congress of the United States appropriated $40,000 to build a new lighthouse on a site only 230 feet northeast of the old one. That much distance was required so the new one could be built before its predecessor was demolished. It was needed because of the many complaints from ship captains that the older light was not visible, and too many ships were being wrecked on the beach. The new lighthouse was to be 167 feet high compared to seventy-four feet—more than twice as high—with a flashing interval of sixty seconds compared to ninety seconds (The interval of flash was later shortened to seven-and-a-half seconds). The new lighthouse could be seen from twenty miles at sea in clear weather, and was built of bricks covered with a yellow cement wash giving it a creamy look. (The present black-and-white bands were created in 1891 to give the Fire Island Light its own color-code). The number of shipwrecks greatly diminished after the new lighthouse went into operation.

On November 1, 1858, this light was turned on for the first time. It became the permanent neighbor of the Surf Hotel and would long outlast the resort. By the following year the first lighthouse was demolished and a new keeper's house was built to the south that could hold three families. The new Fire Island Lighthouse would shine its beacon over the Surf Hotel throughout summer and winter during the dark years of the 1860s, waiting alongside it for better times to return.

Chapter Five
THE SURF HOTEL 1865–1892

Following the end of the Civil War in April 1865 the country slowly began to recover. As its wounds healed, its economic life changed toward peacetime activities again, one of which was the building of railroads everywhere, it seemed, throughout the northeast. And on Long Island plans were made to lay a new railroad line from the Jamaica, Queens terminal of the Long Island Railroad that would serve the South Shore. It was called the South Side Railroad and was incorporated in January 1866. To serve passengers from Brooklyn a line was also built west from Jamaica to a terminal in Williamsburg where a ferry connected to Manhattan. The South Side Railroad eastbound from Jamaica would stop at the many villages along the South Country Road until terminating at Patchogue. This is exactly what David Sammis had been expecting, and it would greatly shorten the trip for guests to the Surf Hotel. As the track began to be laid eastward toward Babylon, he began to plan the expansion of his hotel.

In October 1867 the track reached Babylon only eighteen months after it was started in Jamaica, and on October 28 the first passenger train left the Babylon depot bound for Jamaica. The trip took seventy-five minutes with nine intermediate stops. Passengers were offered two trains a day each way. A huge step had been taken in opening the South Shore to tourists and summer residents.

Getting his guests to the Babylon depot by rail did not satisfy Sammis. He wanted them brought to the ferry dock in the most efficient way, and that meant by trolley. Its proper name was the Babylon Railroad, but it was generally called "the Toonerville Trolley." Guests would get off the South Side

Railroad at the station called "Babylon and Fire Island" which was on the north side of the village. They then would board the trolley waiting at an adjacent track while their trunks and baggage were heaped high on the flatcar behind. When all were loaded, both trolley and flatcar were pulled by a pair of horses. The journey to the ferry was on a single track which ran for one and a half miles down the east side of Deer Park Avenue, across Main Street and down Fire Island Avenue to the steam boat dock. It ran only in the summer from June through September when the Surf Hotel was open. From its beginning in June 1871 it was horse drawn until it was electrified in 1909, after the Surf Hotel had closed for good. For two years a steam car was tried but proved less reliable than the horses. Several trolleys were used over the single track. Sammis had greatly eased the journey by replacing the horse drawn hacks and stages. He also knew he would need faster and more comfortable ferries for the last leg of the trip.

For the first time, in the summer of 1870, Sammis added a second ferry. The Babylon paper reported: "Two steamers, the *Minnie Warren* and *Wilmington*, will ply regularly between Babylon and the Beach connecting with four trains on the S.S. Road [South Side Railroad]. The Surf Hotel will be open for the reception of guests about the first of June."[22] They had replaced the earlier ferries *Bonita* and *Wave*. The paddle-wheel steamer Wilmington had carried guests in 1869, and the following year *Minnie Warren* was added after being renamed *Surf*, serving its namesake for many years to come. A later report from the *New York Evening Express* (1879) said:

> The little steamboat *Surf* is an institution. She used to be called the *Minnie Warren* some years ago and struggled bravely against the strength of the ebb tide in the East River. She starts off quietly, under an easy pressure, runs nicely when the passengers trim the ship and makes the run over the back in about an hour.

Another guest reported:

> I went directly from the depot by the horse-cars to the boat, which was waiting at the dock, and thus made acquaintance with Captain Jacob Thurber, the pilot of the staunch little steamer *Surf*. The captain is a bright, keen, sailorly-

looking man of about thirty-two, one of those men who would inspire you with confidence in his nerve and courage at first sight.[23]

Not everyone felt so secure:

> Then there are some horse cars on which is read *Fire Island*, and taking one of these we are soon in the shores of Great South Bay and aboard the not over clean or commodious steamer *Surf*. She is a steamer, as you are painfully aware if you attempt to go abaft the wheel or loiter too near the engine room, for in the one case you may have a shower of hot spray, and in the other a blast of hot air.[24]

By 1873 Sammis had persuaded the New York State legislature to pass a bill giving him exclusive right to ferry passengers from Babylon to the Surf Hotel. Despite objections from some, this included the right to dock anywhere within two miles of his hotel, which of course meant the Dominy House and any others that might be built over a few miles stretch of land on the beach. If his ferry did not choose to dock at Dominy House, nobody else could provide that service. This restraint would last for ten years and established Sammis with monopoly control over Fire Island Beach for that period. In October 1872, however, he had become a partner with Benjamin Sire in the Dominy House property, so ferry service there was never threatened. (See Chapter 18)

The journey for guests from New York City and from Brooklyn had been made significantly faster and more comfortable than it had been when the Surf Hotel first opened. That fact, together with a steadily improving economic climate, gave Sammis the confidence to substantially increase its capacity as well as to add several new attractions. The twenty years to follow from 1870 to 1890, called the Gilded Age by Mark Twain, became the ideal time to operate a resort hotel in America. Many were built in this era.

"On May 14, 1870, the announcement was made that the Surf Hotel had been greatly enlarged, painted and furnished since the close of the 1869 season and that it would be opened on June 1 for the reception of guests, and that no pains nor expense had been spared to render the house and all its surroundings comfortable, commodious and pleasant to all who would see fit to visit during the season."²⁵ The local paper said that with the large addition to the main building "over 600 guests can repose under its hospitable roof,"²⁶ which was probably an exaggeration.

It is difficult to determine the capacity of the expanded hotel after 1870. A *New York Times* correspondent reported that on an August weekend in 1875, "over three-hundred persons are now in the Surf Hotel," which is certainly a very substantial number. Historian Weeks mentions Sammis's "dream of a palatial summer resort accommodating 400 to 500 guests." A dispatch to the *Saturday Evening Review* in 1879 is quoted here in full, as it is more interesting and probably more accurate coming from a visiting Vermont editor:

> The Surf Hotel kept by Mr. D.S.S. Sammis is located fronting both the ocean and bay. It is 400 feet long, three stories, and surrounded by a thirty-foot balcony. Two covered walks run down to the steamboat landing on the bay side and one also to the ocean shore…The dining room is a large building located by itself away from the hotel and connected with it by covered walks. At the ocean beach is a long veranda, which is lighted up by street lamps. Ample bathing houses are also near.
>
> "The regular accommodations for guests is 500, but on a Sunday and holidays, when extra exertion is made, full double that number is entertained. Many of New York's most prominent and wealthy men have their wives and children here and come and spend Sunday here themselves. A number return every night, which is in no way difficult, as the trip, including steamer ride, is less than two hours.²⁷

One might conclude that although the Surf possibly could have held 500 guests for the night, 300 was a better estimate of attendance on a busy summer weekend. Many more would come to the annual balls or for special parties.

Improvements to the interior of the main three-story building were also made in 1869–70, as well as its enlargement. These were commented on in a report to the *Home Journal* in July 30, 1882:

> Not only is the mode of travel improved, the hotel itself shows improvement. What was once a scant and skimping

office is now a broad and beautiful reception room, handsomely furnished and decorated. The billiard room is twice the size it was, and the third of a mile of plank walk to the ocean is doubled in width. Many of the rooms are newly furnished and the beds, some of which years ago were a trifle hard and unyielding, are now soft and luxurious. Mr. Sammis, like the rest of us, is getting older, but...he keeps abreast of the times.

There were also several separate buildings on the hotel grounds. Mentioned in the earlier dispatch was the building containing the large dining room and the kitchen, which was also used as a ballroom. In addition there were nine cottages containing forty-five rooms for guests together with four with names: Albany Cottage, Townsend Cottage, Whitney Cottage, and Coudert Cottage, the latter three named after regular guests. Albany Cottage was by far the largest, holding seventy people on several floors. It became famous because of its patronage by noted political leaders and legislators. Thus, it was estimated that, including 130 people on the staff, the Surf Hotel could accommodate and feed 830 people for the night once all the cottages had been completed.

Near the ocean there was a bathing pavilion and many bathhouses. On the bay side was a 300-foot dock that could accommodate the two ferries and any guest yachts. All the structures were connected with boardwalks, most of which were covered to protect guests in inclement weather. A guest who returned after a ten-year absence commented:

A covered walk to the surf has been erected, nearly a mile long; new bathing houses, this because the old ones, with the pavilion, were swept away last spring in the great storm which sent the *Spartan* ashore; the new ones have cost him about $1,500. There are other changes. I find the lighthouse much further inshore, and they tell me the island is reversing the order of things and is encroaching on the Atlantic at the rate of several yards a year, and on the bay side the water is all the time getting shallower.

It may be that at no distant date the island will again become a peninsula or 'point' as Long Island historians say it was once, and that the original Fire Island, which lies buried under the waters of the Atlantic, will again come to the surface.[28]

An interesting feature of the main building was the two cupolas atop the roof. One of these was used as an observatory to watch the ships that passed eastbound and westbound. From the height of the cupola one could see over ten miles out to sea in clear weather. In 1879 it was reported:

There is an observatory on the top of the hotel, the place from which the first-sight reports of the European steamers are sent. It is glassed on all sides, and pigeon-hole boxes are arranged for a sweeping range of spyglasses. The telegraph lines which link Fire Island to the entire world, and which are never cut off from circuit with the Western Union office in New York are located in this square sitting room, where the gentlemen sometimes lounge and smoke and the ladies visit, despite the "No Admittance" sign at the foot of the stairway. Mr. William H. Temple is the chief operator in charge and Mr. Keegan, his assistant, helps him do the sighting of ships, and knows all the secrets of the office in the messages flashed over the wires to him.[29]

Although the wireless room was used to notify New York of the sighting of ships and their arrival times, it was also the fastest means of communication for guests.

Ship sighting from the cupola became so advantageous to its customers that in 1885 the Fire Island Observatory was built by Western Union. The space in the cupola was no longer adequate and had likely become a nuisance to the hotel guests. The new marine observatory was located north of the Surf's bathhouses and a quarter mile east of the lighthouse with a wide and unobstructed view of the Atlantic Ocean.

It was a plain, square structure, solidly constructed with heavy timbers securely braced and with guys at each corner made fast to heave anchors in that beach. The two lower stories were used as a dwelling by Observer Peter Keegan and his family and the square upper room, sixty feet from the ground, commanded an extensive view in all directions.[30]

The Western Union Telegraph Tower was manned around the clock all year long to report the arrival of ships to New York Harbor. In 1898 it was raised from a five-story tower to an eight-story tower 75 feet high and the living quarters were enlarged. Joseph Doughty, the observer from 1897 to 1920, raised a family of three children in the watchtower. The addition was built because Western Union had competition that year from the Postal Telegraph Company's new 75 foot iron tower, located a half mile to the east near present day Kismet. Being located to the east Postal Telegraph hoped to sight west-bound ocean liners before their rival and to get the news to New York first. Occasionally, of course, one tower or the other would miss a ship altogether, giving the other company a big coup. Eventually they began to tip each other off—cooperation had replaced competition.

On the top floor of both towers were huge spyglasses that could be elevated to scan the horizon and follow the approach of ships. The lenses were close to thirty inches in diameter and through them sailors on the Fire Island Lightship could be seen ten miles away after it had been stationed there in 1896. It was particularly important to be able to identify the newest, fastest passenger liners of that era, which required considerable skill even with the aid of lenses. The Western Union's Peter Keegan, its observer from 1876 to 1897, became a master of that skill. In 1886 the *Brooklyn Eagle* correspondent described him thus:

> There is probably no other man in America who can fill his position today. When he takes a leave of absence, which is seldom, the observatory is closed, the company having no man they would dare trust to make observations. It may at first thought appear singular that such is the fact, but consider a moment: the tracks of the ocean steamers on an average are thirteen miles from the observatory. At that distance the outlines of a vessel are very indistinct, except in very clear weather, and at times the untrained eye can hardly distinguish any object whatever. Then think of the large number of steamers to be recognized and their names correctly reported, for there must be no mistake.... Mr. Keegan, therefore, must not make a mistake, and he rarely does. But how can he know all the vessels?
>
> Only once has Mr. Keegan been able to read the name of a vessel passing his station and that was a few years ago when the *Amerique* came within three miles of shore.... He could tell the name quicker by seeing her masts and smokestacks eighteen miles from shore than by seeing her hull, deck, and rigging [from close by].

Mr. Keegan is an intelligent man, reading many books during long vigils, He is, of course, greatly aided by knowing when to expect certain steamers, but it often happens that two steamers of the same line are expected at about the same time, and then his knowledge of minute details comes into play. For instance, on one smoke stack of the *Servia* is a square white mark, while on other Cunarders the mark is oblong. Certain vessels carry their sails in a particular manner and others have heavy rigging. One steamer has a derrick in a certain place, and there are a hundred other distinguishing marks to the trained observer. By careful observation Mr. Keegan has noted all these details. Each line has its own course. From one porthole on the lookout room at a certain angle he watches for a steamer of the Guion line, and from another porthole the *Inman*, and so on.

Every steamer signals its name to the Fire Island station by flags, but often its approach is reported an hour before this is done. Mr. Keegan does not like to trust flag signals for at times they are very deceptive, the atmosphere causing certain colors to appear different from what they are."[31]

So Peter Keegan became the indispensable master observer for Western Union. Not long after he retired, however, an Italian inventor, Guglielmo Marconi, discovered how to transmit messages by radio waves. From a shack on Fire Island Avenue in Babylon, Long Island, in 1901, he contacted a ship at sea off the Fire Island beach and it responded. The wireless was born and soon thereafter replaced the Western Union cable. A Fire Island radio tower was built in 1907 and for a time co-existed with its older rivals. In 1918 the Western Union tower was taken over by the U.S. Navy for two years before closing for good in 1920. The Postal Telegraph tower closed that year as well.

By the summer of 1870, the expansion of the Surf Hotel was complete, accessibility for its guests had been greatly improved, and the economic life of New York was on an upswing for a time. The Surf could handle as many as 400 to 500 guests, a very large number. Thus, it is appropriate to consider why people of means would want to come there. By then there were several other resorts in the New York area, although none were within fifty miles of the city on an ocean beach. The Marine Pavilion in Far Rockaway had burned down in 1864 and the large hotels in the Brighton Beach and Long Beach areas had not yet been built.

The Surf Hotel promoted its features in an advertisement in the spring of 1884 by listing eleven reasons for a visit. They are listed below with some explanatory comments by the author:

1. Its pure sea breezes, always cool and refreshing [predominantly southwest];
2. Excellent beach, which affords superb surf bathing; also still bathing, if preferred to surf [the latter in the Great South Bay];
3. At the very doors of the hotel you may revel in the sand or sea;
4. Sailing and fishing can be enjoyed to perfection in the waters of the Great South Bay and Ocean;
5. It is the only place near New York where those suffering from hay fever or "rose cold" can obtain relief [Mrs. Herman Melville suffered from hay fever—see Chapter Six];
6. A certain relief for catarrh [the common cold];
7. For children it is paradise;
8. Here may be enjoyed all the beneficial effects of the Ocean, without the discomforts of a sea voyage;
9. The air is always cool at Fire Island [the maximum temperature of the wind off the ocean is 70∞F];
10. The hotel is supplied with piped water [from wells to the Long Island aquifer], has excellent drainage, is lighted with gas, and has accommodation for 400 guests. Also ten cottages in connection with the hotel;
11. It is the "place of places" in which to get rid of chills and malarial fever [it was then thought that a cool environment had some beneficial effect on malaria].

Although this advertisement was promotional, it was by and large accurate, though it of course did not mention aspects of life on Fire Island that were unpleasant or hazardous, namely mosquitoes and storms.

Some of the guests at the Surf Hotel made interesting comments about life there and about its host David Sammis. He was very much a presence at the hotel, with a personal touch that was felt at all times. A repeat visitor in 1879 said:

"A peculiarly home-like place is Sammis's Surf Hotel, and those who know the way there pay good prices for staying within his domains. He is a pleasant monarch to live under, and good nature is not sacrificed to the cares of his establishment. [...] There is a feeling of relaxation from care, and of prospective comfort which the visitor experiences in actuality when he knows Sammis."[32]

"Host Sammis is looking hardly a day older than when I saw him last—the same jovial smile and hearty manner greets the return of old patrons."[33]

"There is a freedom of restraint at the Surf Hotel which amounts to almost a homelike feeling. The same people come here year after year, and though Mr. Sammis welcomes new guests every day of the season, no objectionable person could possibly obtain a foothold at his hotel. For perfect ease, relief for the weary mind, and rest for the body, there is no place like Fire Island, and for the host—who shall surpass the landlord of the Surf Hotel?"[34]

"Mr. Sammis's usual costume was a brown or gray suit, and he chiefly affected in cold weather a cape overcoat. He seldom wore anything on his head but a silk hat, occasionally exchanging the "topper" for a gray felt one of corresponding height. He was always a dressy man and wore broadcloth even when "bossing" a group of laborers or driving about town overlooking his property."[35]

There were many activities for guests. Among the most popular was the wonderful fishing. It had been the fishing for blues that had first attracted people from New York to the bay and to the Fire Island Lighthouse in the 1830s, as has been noted. Although the inlet had moved westward, it was still very easy to reach from the Surf Hotel and the fish were still plentiful. A guest commented, "A score of tidy catboats are moored at the pier and parties frequently start at daybreak, or soon after, and sail out at the ocean, taking lunch and returning only in time for supper. Yesterday our boat brought back between forty and fifty fine fish, and among them were two or three ten pounders."[36] In addition to the bluefish, Spanish mackerel were a popular catch in that era.

These could be taken in the bay if it was too rough to venture out to the ocean. And if one did not care for fishing, the catboats at the Surf were available to sail around the bay, one of the most protected waters with fair breezes within fifty miles of New York City.

Other activities were billiards, bowling in a ten-pin alley west of the bar room, and outdoor tennis. "Mrs. E. Norton Hasbrouck of Babylon, Sammis's granddaughter, remembered the Surf Hotel tennis court as having a sturdy concrete base. It was apparently given a macadam surfacing, as beach visitors of long afterwards can attest."[37] The court was situated to the north of the main building and was protected from the southwest winds.

On Sunday mornings at 11:00AM, Divine Service was held in the parlor for those guests who chose to attend. It was a Protestant service led either by a minister who was invited to preach a sermon or occasionally by a layperson if no minister was present. In that era it was common to have religious services in hotels and blue laws were adhered to strictly.

Although the Surf did not feature too many scheduled entertainments for its guests, there was usually dancing on Saturday evenings in the dining room.

"The season has been a very good one, so far, since the 4th of July," it was reported. "Yesterday 'Uncle David' [Sammis] astonished the hotel and to tell the truth, I believe himself too, by appearing in a new suit of yellow, cut in the most approved style, and discarding his older color, dark blue....

We had two or three very pleasant [parties] this summer, the later and most successful one being last Saturday evening. The favors were very elegant and appropriate, having been under the immediate supervision of the Misses Brandreth of Sing Sing [a town of the Hudson River later called Ossining]. Dancing was begun at 9 o'clock and kept up until the office clock warned the leader that Sunday was at hand [Sunday blue laws were then in effect].

The gentleman just referred to performed the arduous task of leading in a most satisfactory manner, introducing some original figures, which were heartily applauded by the dancers and the large audience of guests who lined the walls of the commodious parlor.[38]

Usually near the end of each summer in August a masquerade ball was held in the large dining hall, decorated for that special occasion. It was the climax of the season, a party attended by many who were not overnight guests of the hotel. A correspondent of the *New York Times* attended the event in August 16, 1875, and reported:

> Over three hundred persons are now in the Surf Hotel, and certainly there has been no year when arrangements for visitors were more thoroughly looked after. Mr. Williams, the steward, has once more proved himself an excellent chief of the commissariat, and considering that everything for the table, large or small, has to be brought from the mainland—chiefly from New York—the supplies may be recorded as wonderfully good.

It should be emphasized how difficult and expensive it was to supply the Surf Hotel with fresh food during the summer for such a large number of people. The refrigeration alone cost Sammis $2,000 to purchase ice packed in sawdust and brought from Maine by schooner.

> On Saturday night there was a masked ball at the hotel, and considering that it had been got up in a very short time, it was a really brilliant success. The ladies showed their usual skill in dress by constructing costumes which were either amusing or graceful, and often both. Miss Diossy had made a charming dress for herself out of newspapers. If the attractions of a newspaper depend on what is put inside it, Miss Diossy produced the most interesting journal I have seen for some time. I wish a newspaper always looked so well. This young lady may be truly said to have excelled most of us who have perhaps been longer at the work. Miss L. Sammis made herself into a lovely representative of "morning." One could wish so bright a morning as that never to pass into the glow of mid-day or the melancholy of night. Her brother appeared in the more prosaic character of a French cook. Mrs. Dr. Draper (who had, I believe, kindly interested herself in getting up the masquerade) was a distinguished-looking Belgian peasant and Mrs. G. Terry appeared as a French *bonne*. Some of the other ladies who took parts in the ball were—Miss Brandreth, as Folly; Miss C. Pease, a handsome sorceress—highly dangerous, I should say, to all who are brought within reach of her magic spells; Miss J. Pease, a shepherdess, and there are few who would not wish to be among her flock; Miss Lighthite, (two), as

Scotch lassies; Miss Carslake, a nun; Mrs. Terry, a lady of the period; Miss A. Sammis, a postulant. Among the gentlemen were Mr. Lighthite who, in character of a colored boot-black, added much to the fun of the evening. Mr. Mitchell, as a footman, was also very amusing. There were several other gentlemen, whose names I did not happen to hear. At 10:30 refreshments were served by Mr. Sammis, and the dancing was kept up till near midnight. On this occasion, as on many others, the visitors were indebted to Mr. Austin for kindly volunteering to play the piano.[39]

It was customary in the Gilded Age to celebrate special events with a masked ball or masquerade. The party that Sammis planned for the end of summer was typical of those found in other resorts and was used as well by affluent people such as Mrs. Astor and Mrs. Vanderbilt.

In fairness it should be pointed out that there were two conditions on Fire Island that were never mentioned in any of the advertisements of the Surf Hotel and only rarely in the newspapers: the infestation of mosquitoes and the threat of storms or even hurricanes.

In the nineteenth century before the great population growth that would follow, the Great South Bay's north side was a very rural area with villages only along the South Country Road. The road ran east and west a mile or two inland from the shore of the bay, which was marshland along its entire length. Only where village docks had been built, such as the Babylon ferry dock, was the line of marshes broken by landfill. This topography created the ideal breeding ground for the mosquito. They also bred on Fire Island in the marshes that existed north of the barrier beach. And from June through September—the resort season—they were a plague. The efforts to control the plague were minimal, although it was thought that cutting grass closely would help. At the Surf Hotel the prevailing southwest wind off the ocean would keep the pests away during the day, but in the evening they would return, keeping guests inside for the most part. The *New York Times* reporter said:

Since the sudden visitation of mosquitoes which fell upon the place last year, some nervousness has been felt lest there should be a repetition of the plague but, although in

the evening mosquitoes do put in an appearance, it is quite
easy to keep them out of one's rooms, and for weeks together
not one is seen. They have never been so bad this year as
I have seen them at Babylon and some parts of Fire Island.
This year the mosquitoes have been unusually thick everywhere, even in New York City, and I am only surprised that
there are not more here. Mr. Sammis has, however, kept all
the grass near the hotel well plowed in, and the holes filled
with sand, The occasional nuisance of mosquitoes is not for
a moment to be set against the advantage of perfectly good
air and a fresh sea-breeze all summer.[40]

Mosquitoes were a nuisance, as the writer said, but only
that against the many advantages that the Surf had to offer.
The threat of storms was much more serious, and some did
occur during the time David Sammis operated the hotel.
Although not as serious as those that occurred before and
after that time, they did cause damage. They were also a
concern to guests; since there could be no warning of a
storm's arrival in that era, guests could not be evacuated
on the two ferries.

On September 18, 1876, a severe gale was reported that
caused damage to the ferry *Surf*, whose anchor had dragged
and was thus beached in Fire Island. A day later a guest perished: "John Crosby of New York was drowned in the surf at
Fire Island. Mrs. Crosby and a daughter were the only ones
on the beach at the time, and before other assistance arrived
the swimmer had drifted beyond reach. A reward of $250 has
been offered for the body to be delivered to D.S.S. Sammis."[41]

A more serious storm occurred on August 20, 1879, which
could have well been labeled a hurricane today. The Babylon
paper reported:

The storm of Monday afternoon and night was the most
severe that has been known in this section, at this season
of the year for 25 years. It was so entirely unexpected [as
was the hurricane of 1938], that it caught all the boatmen
unawares and some of the light crafts at Fire Island got a
severe drubbing. At the Surf Hotel about 25 feet of the roof
to the covered walk west of the bar room was blown over
on the ten-pin alley, doing no damage to the alley. The bulkhead walk was torn to pieces. The dock was uninjured.
Several of the Surf's catboats were damaged and had to be

sent to the mainland for repair. The sloop owned by Lawrence
Newins of Patchogue, who supplies the Surf Hotel with vegetables etc. was laying at the dock and will be a total loss.
The steamer 'Surf' skipped the Monday night trip, and
lay at the Babylon dock, receiving no injury.
Tuesday morning after the storm things in the vicinity of the Surf Hotel looked pretty dreary. Seaweed was
piled on the bulkhead from 4 to 6 feet high and was filled
with boards, fish lines and general wreck stuff. At the time
of writing, everything has been righted up, and the place
wears its usual smiling aspect.[42]

Both storms occurred during the summer season; fortunately
the 1879 one passed through on a Monday when many weekend guests had already departed. Still, it was a frightening
experience for those in residence.

The worst storm of all during the Sammis years was a
winter gale that arrived when the Surf Hotel was empty, with
only the Fire Island Lighthouse keepers and the Western
Union Telegraph operators in their houses nearby. Had this
storm come during the summer or fall it would have surely
been called a hurricane. However winter storms do not have
the tight circular airflow around the low-pressure center,
known as an "eye," that characterizes hurricanes. They can
be just as damaging to the beach and even more so if they
last for several days, as did the 1962 winter storm.

The Babylon paper reported on New Years Day in 1881:
The storm of Sunday night last did considerable damage
along the south shore of Long Island. At Fire Island the sea
broke solid across the beach between the Surf Hotel and
the lighthouse, a large cabin from some stranded vessel,
and much wreckage being washed over into the bay. At one
time the hotel itself was in imminent danger of being washed
away. The pavilion at the surf was partly undermined by
the sea, and all the bathing houses belonging to the hotel,
numbering about 100, were swept away, and the materials
of which they were composed strewn along the shore. Among
the debris thrown up from the sea was the hull of an old
steamer, of about 1,200 tons burden, that no one has been
able to recognize. What vessel it is (or was) will probably
always remain a mystery. A number of telegraph poles,
forming the land connection with the Fire Island and
Babylon submarine cable, were washed out, thus breaking

communication, but no damage was done to the submerged cable. The tides were higher in the bay and along the outer shore than noted before in several years.[43]

In spite of mosquitoes and the threat of storms, the experience of guests at the Surf was very positive. It was perhaps best expressed by a guest who came in August of 1878:

On Sunday the surf was splendid and I found myself running around on the beach like a very schoolboy let loose... The sunset was glorious on Sunday night. I sat on the bay side of the island and watched his splendid departure... Very shortly after the moon appeared above the horizon like a flaming ball of fire, and her advent I saw from the ocean's edge.

Shortly after, some of the guests organized a children's meeting in the parlor, and the little ones ranged around the piano in a semi-circle and sang some of their hymns... The people here all seem to be thoroughly at home and enjoy themselves after their individual tastes.[44]

This pastoral scene of the nineteenth century still speaks to those who come to Fire Island today.

As the Surf Hotel grew in popularity in the 1870s it became a stopping off point for the large private sailing yachts that often raced in the Atlantic Ocean on the America Cup's race course between Sandy Hook, New Jersey, and the whistling buoy off the Fire Island Lighthouse. Some of these had been built at Alonzo Smith's shipyard in Islip across the bay, and several were under the command of Bay Shore's and Islip's famous sailing masters. Seen at the hotel's bayside anchorage on July 4, 1873, was the centerboard schooner *Clio*, owned by John R. Platt, a member of the Olympic Club of Bay Shore. In command of the vessel was Samuel Greenwood, the sailing master. *Clio* and her better-known rivals *Gracie* and *Irene* were a part of a huge flotilla of 140 sailing craft that had assembled to celebrate the holiday "with their white sails and gay streamers,"[45] a very picturesque sight to behold.

Clio was typical of these large sailing yachts: seventy feet long, fifty-eight feet on the waterline, and drawing only six feet with the centerboard up, allowing her to sail in the bay albeit with only one or two sails up. In the ocean the board would be extended down seventeen feet, with the schooner under full sail with its two topsails and a balloon jib measuring sixty feet at the foot. Inside were three large staterooms all well furnished for great comfort. *Clio* was said to cost Mr. Platt $9,000.

During the 4th of July the following year (1874) the schooner *Comet* was seen lying off the Surf's dock. Ten feet or so longer than *Clio*, she had been built for William H. Langley of the New York Yacht Club and was launched at Alonzo Smith's yard on Islip's Orowoc Creek in May 1874 amid great fanfare. Many of Islip's captains were present for the occasion, including Captains Hank Haff, John Ellsworth and John Havens. The yachts in the harbor were dressed with bunting and flags.

After several trials, *Comet* joined the racing fleet that summer off Fire Island with considerable success—so much so that she was challenged in October by the schooner *Magic* in a high-stakes match race. *Magic* at eighty-four feet overall was the larger boat and had won the America's Cup in 1870 under a previous owner. In 1874 she was owned by William T. Garner of Bay Shore and sailed by Captain Nathaniel Clock of Islip, who would win the cup in 1881 with the sloop *Mischief*. The *Magic-Comet* yacht race was held on October 13, 1874, over the New York Yacht Club course between Staten Island and Fire Island. *Magic's* greater size and Clock's greater experience were too much for *Comet* to overcome. Garner was said to have won a fortune on that high-stakes race.

Other yachts often seen at the Surf's anchorage were the schooners *Vixen*, owned by Garner's brother-in-law Francis C. Lawrance and sailed by Captain Samuel Gibson, both of Bay Shore; the sloop *Fanny*, owned by John D. Prince and sailed by Captains John Havens and then Hank Haff, both of Islip; and the yacht *Onward* owned by Adjutant General Fred Townsend of Albany, who was a regular occupant of a cottage at the Surf Hotel.

However, not all large, visiting boats were welcome at the hotel dock. Late in the summer of 1882 as the season was winding down, a large steamboat named *Sirius*, under the command of Captain Moses Longstreet, appeared through the Fire Island Inlet and signaled a request to dock. Unbeknown to the dock master, she had departed New York City four hours earlier with 700 passengers onboard for a day's outing, all expecting to be fed and entertained at the Surf. It was said that Sammis was aghast; he was not at all prepared and did not favor large groups of day-trippers. However he cautiously admitted them to the dining room where they were offered meat and potatoes. Apparently they had expected fish and began complaining. The staff became upset, saying such things as: "You can have nothing else," "We don't get up dinner for excursionists," "This hotel is run for guests," and "We didn't want you to come here." Finally Sammis, annoyed at the furor, said, "I don't want excursionists at all. You'll have to be satisfied with what you got. If you don't like it, go elsewhere."[46] The guests were frustrated, but there was nowhere else to go. As they left the dining room for their steam boat, Sammis stood by the door and collected $1 from each of the 300 excursionists who had obtained seats in his dining room. When all were back aboard *Sirius*, a full meal of chicken, roast beef, lobster salad, coffee, cakes and pies were ready and quickly devoured by the hungry group who docked at New York City at 8:00PM. Sammis had not made friends that day, but he knew that his regular clients did not want to be disturbed by day-trippers from the city.

In the late 1870s while David Sammis's Surf Hotel was enjoying great popularity as the only seaside resort on Long Island's Atlantic beaches, another man had the vision of building resort hotels and giving them much improved rail service and more active promotion. His timing was excellent as the effects of the Depression of 1873 had passed and vacationers had begun to flock to resorts in greater numbers. His name was Austin Corbin.

A decade younger than Sammis, Corbin came from an entirely different background. He was born and educated in New Hampshire, graduated from the prestigious Harvard Law School, and went out west to establish a banking busi-

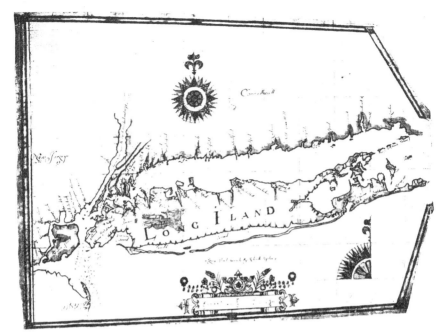

Map of Long Island by Robert Ryder circa 1675. Note that the South Beach is broken by an inlet with an island north of it, both in the approximate location of the Fire Island Inlet today. *Courtesy of John Carter Brown Library at Brown University.*

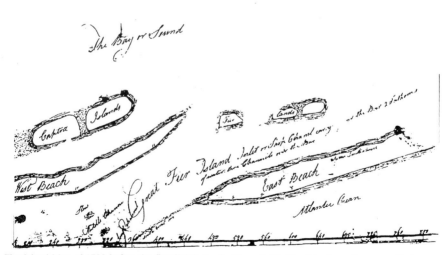

Fire Island Map of 1798 before the first lighthouse had been built. Fire Island was known as East Beach then. The map made by surveyor Samuel Wheeler. *Courtesy of* The Fire Island Tide *newspaper.*

Dominy House 1844 to 1903. This is the only known photograph taken in 1902, the year before it was destroyed by fire. *Courtesy of* The Commodore's Story *by Ralph Middleton Monroe.*

The Greek revival style Marine Pavilion, constructed on Rockaway Beach in 1834, was the earliest resort hotel on the Great South Beach of Long Island. *Courtesy of the Brooklyn Historical Society.*

David S. S. Sammis of Brooklyn built the Surf Hotel in 1856. He owned and operated it until 1892. *A formal photograph, courtesy of Carl A. Starace and the* Long Island Forum.

The second Fire Island Lighthouse pictured here was built in 1858 and painted yellow, giving it a creamy look. In 1891, it was repainted with the familiar black and white stripes, a designation particular to it among the east coast lighthouses. *Courtesy of the Point O' Woods Library.*

Castle Conklin, Captree Island, was an early hotel near Fire Island Inlet which was frequented by boats fishing for blue fish. *Courtesy of the Brooklyn Historical Society.*

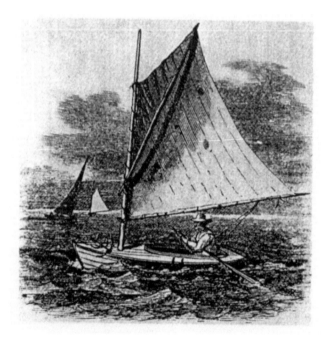

Blue fishing was popular with guests at the Surf Hotel, Dominy House and other small hostelries. Occasionally boats were sailed single-handed but more often the boat captain took out several guests. *Courtesy of the Brooklyn Historical Society and of The Old Print Shop, New York.*

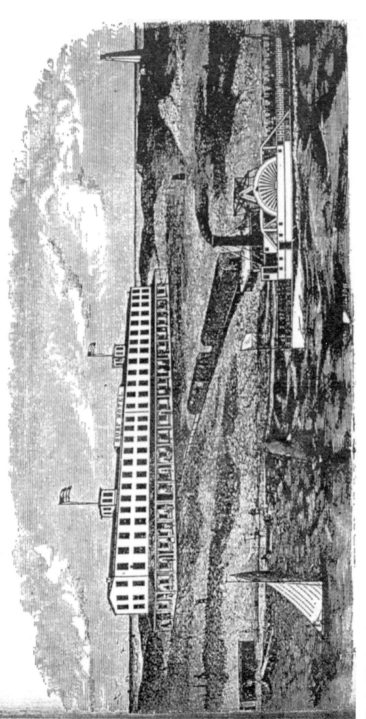

The Surf Hotel as pictured in an 1857 advertisement. It already had bathhouses and a covered walk. *Courtesy Carl A. Starace and the* Long Island Forum.

After the railroad reached Babylon in 1868, the Surf Hotel expanded and prospered. Above is a photograph of the first station house at Babylon reassuring customers who desired to get off the train for Fire Island. *Courtesy of the archives of Ron Ziel.*

The Surf Hotel pictured after the addition of a wing at right. Note two tennis players on the concrete court. *Courtesy of the Fullerton Collection, Suffolk County Historical Society.*

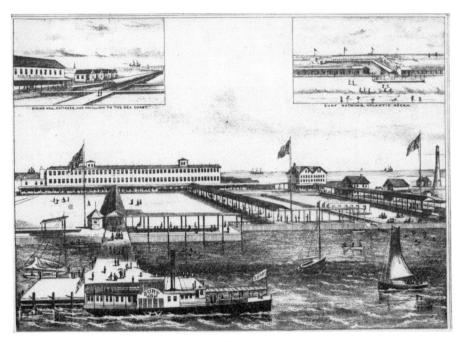

A sketch of the vast Surf Hotel complex in the 1870s with the steamer *Surf* at the pier. Note the two cupolas on top of the main building from where ships at sea were sighted by the Western Union Telegraph office.

Sail boats tied up at the Surf Hotel dock circa 1880s. Note the dresses worn by the ladies of that era on sporting occasions.

Looking east from the top of the Fire Island Lighthouse circa 1900. In the foreground is the Surf Hotel complex with the four story Albany cottage in the center. In the background is the Dominy House and the private home of Benjamin Sire to its right. *Courtesy of the Fire Island Lighthouse Preservation Society.*

The Western Union Telegraph tower built in 1876 south and west of the Surf Hotel. It was five stories high, at first, to spot ships coming from Europe and to advise the Port of New York by cable of their arrival. *Courtesy of the Babylon Public Library.*

A higher tower was added later creating an eight story look-out. Closed in 1920, it was destroyed in the hurricane of 1938. *Courtesy of the Fire Island Lighthouse Preservation Society.*

Rapid Transit to Oak Island, Babylon, L. I.

From the railroad station, passengers took the rapid transit, a horse-drawn trolley of the Babylon Railroad Company which ran on tracks to the Babylon Steamboat dock. *Courtesy of* Images of America.

The Babylon Steamboat dock owned by David S.S. Sammis. Ferries to the Surf Hotel and later to Oak Beach, Oak Island, Cedar Beach, Muncie Island and Gilgo Beach departed from the dock in picture circa 1908. *Photograph by Henry Otto Korten, Nassau County Museum.*

The paddle-wheel steamboat ferry *Ripple* took passengers from the Babylon dock to the Surf Hotel following the demise of the steamer *Surf*. When New York State acquired her in 1892. the name was changed to *James W. Wadsworth. Photograph by Carl A. Starace.*

Herman Melville spent several of his last summers at the Surf Hotel. It was said that he wrote parts of his final novel, *Billy Budd,* there. His wife came to avoid hay fever which had plagued her in the summer elsewhere. Melville died in 1891. *Courtesy* The New York Times.

Grover Cleveland, one of three United States presidents who stayed at the Surf Hotel. The others were James Garfield before his presidency and his successor, Chester A. Arthur.

Peter Cooper
American Manufacturer & Philanthropist
1791-1883

New Yorker Peter Cooper, inventor, manufacturer, philanthropist and a guest at the Surf Hotel.

U. S. Life Saving Station, Oak Island Beach, N. Y.

The Oak Island Beach U.S. Life-Saving Station typical of those built along the beach and operated by crews of that service from 1871 to 1915. They were located from three to six miles apart along the Great South Beach. *Courtesy of* Images of America.

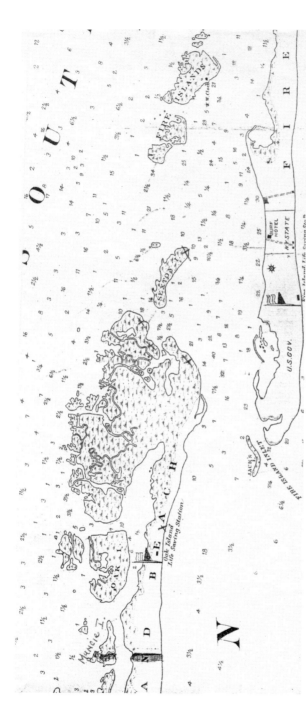

A map by E. Belcher Hyde dated 1896 showing Muncie Island on the left to East Fire Island on the far right. By this date there were 15 private houses on Oak Island; the Havermeyer Point House (formerly the Armory), Jesse Conklin's place and the WA-Wa-Yanda Club on Captree Island; and the Short Beach Club on Sexton Island.

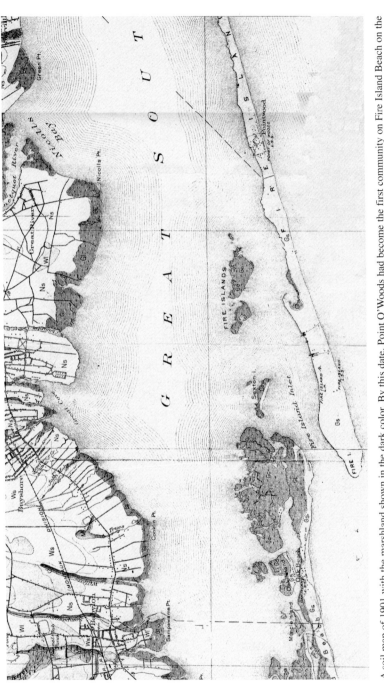

A soil map of 1901 with the marshland shown in the dark color. By this date, Point O'Woods had become the first community on Fire Island Beach on the right. Sampawams Point on the left marks the entrance to the Babylon town dock where ferries departed for the Surf Hotel.

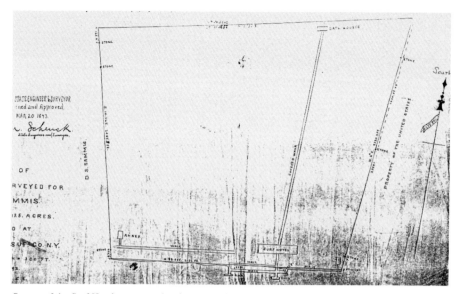

Survey of the Surf Hotel property when it was purchased by New York State in March 1893

During the cholera scare in September 1892, quarantined passengers aboard *Cepheus* were prevented from landing at the dock of the Surf Hotel by enraged residents of Babylon pointing shot guns in the air. *Photograph from* Harper's Weekly.

An outline map showing the location of the ocean liner *Normannia* anchored in the Lower Bay at the left and the Surf Hotel at the far right. *Cepheus* took 600 passengers from the ship to the hotel twice before they were allowed to disembark. *Photograph from* Harper's Weekly.

Joyous passengers of *Cepheus* coming ashore at the dock of the Surf Hotel after 72 hours of hardship. *Drawing from the* New York Herald *September 14, 1892.*

ness in Iowa before returning to New York after the Civil War. In New York he founded his own banking company and specialized in re-organizing railroads that were in trouble. It is said that while visiting an ailing son in a small hotel in Coney Island, Corbin walked along the ocean beach there and saw the potential of Long Island's ocean frontage. There is no evidence that he had been a guest at the Surf Hotel, but it is quite likely, and he surely knew about its success from newspaper articles.

In 1876 Corbin built a rail line from Bay Ridge in Brooklyn to Coney Island, the east end of which was known as Manhattan Beach, and followed that with two huge hotels, first the Manhattan Beach Hotel in 1877 and then the Oriental Hotel in 1880—as well as a theater, stadium, and bandstand. Not far away was the Sheepshead Bay racetrack, which brought many patrons to the hotels. At last David Sammis had competition. On August 2, 1880, the *New York Times* said:

> It is only within the last four or five years, or since the success of the Manhattan Beach enterprise, that the importance and value of these beaches began to be appreciated. First after the Manhattan Beach came the Brighton Beach [not a Corbin hotel], which also proved a great success; then came the mammoth Rockaway enterprise [not Corbin either] on which $700,000 has been expended during the past years and $300,000 more is to be spent on its completion. To the eastward of Rockaway lies Long Beach, which opened for the first time this summer [owned by Austin Corbin] after an expenditure of $500,000.

The Rockaway Beach Hotel (mentioned above), located near the site of the original Marine Pavilion that had burned down a decade earlier, advertised itself as the largest hotel in the world with 1,188 feet of facade, 100,000 square feet of piazza, and a 1,300-foot ocean pier. These piers, on which small amusements and eateries were set, were the forerunners of today's amusement parks and were modeled on the famous Brighton pier on the south coast of England, a popular Victorian seaside spa.

Corbin owned these three large hotels—which he expected to fill the following summer—in 1880, just as the Long Island

Railroad declared bankruptcy due to losses from poor management, shoddy equipment, and unreliable service. Putting
together a syndicate of investors, Corbin persuaded the court-
appointed receiver to award the railroad to him and his
investors based on his experience with troubled railroads and
his knowledge of Long Island. On January 1, 1881, he was
named President. He had said to the press a month earlier:
> "I have always believed in Long Island, in its advantages
> as a place of residence, in its agricultural productiveness,
> in the attractiveness of its summer resorts and in its value
> for railroad purposes. All the island needs is development
> and now that development is going to take place. What the
> railroad needs is to be managed as a sensible man would
> manage his own business. The demands of travel must be
> fully complied with and the trains must run rapidly and
> on time....
> "I propose to make the south side of Long Island the
> greatest watering place in the world. Its natural beauties
> and advantages are so great that the improvement of the
> whole stretch of coast is as certain to come as the world is
> to stand. I have lived there for eight years and I know
> whereof I speak when I say that the climate, the scenery,
> and the natural attractions are unsurpassed in any part of
> this country or Europe. I have not a particle of doubt that
> within ten years the south side from Coney Island to
> Montauk Point will be boarded by a continuous chain of
> seaside resorts." The Long Island Railroad began to reflect
Corbin's tremendous enthusiasm by publishing brochures
describing the various resorts on the South Shore and how
they could be reached easily by rail. Some of these resort
hotels were built by Corbin's own Long Island Improvement
Co.—such as the Manhattan Beach Hotel in Coney Island.[47]

Corbin followed his take-over of the Long Island Railroad by
building another new hotel, this time in Babylon itself—
Sammis's hometown—near the train station. He called it the
Argyle. He was getting close to the Surf and offering a resort
experience not on the ocean but on a lake in Babylon village.
Would the Argyle take guests away from the Surf?

The Argyle was completed in 1882. It offered 350 rooms
for 700 guests on three floors of the main building, fourteen
separate cottages and a casino for entertainment, dancing

and dining, but not gambling. Boating and fishing in the lake were also popular activities, but of course bluefishing and ocean swimming were not possible due to its inland location. Sammis had no cause to worry. The Argyle was only a third full during the first summer and never came close to attracting enough guests to make a profit. In 1891 it was sold at auction and in 1897 it closed for good and was torn down a few years later.

For the most part Austin Corbin and David Sammis had amicable relations. The Argyle never threatened the business of the Surf Hotel and Sammis was pleased with the improving performance of the Long Island Railroad. Only after the Surf was sold to the State of New York in 1893 did they disagree over the use of the Babylon connecting railroad to the ferry, which Sammis wanted to continue. Corbin, however, refused to allow its track and platform use on his Long Island Railroad. By then Sammis was seventy-five and near the end of his life. Corbin remained president of the Long Island Railroad until his sudden death in an accident in 1896. He had succeeded in his goals of turning the railroad into a first-class operation and developing and promoting the Long Island economy, particularly its tourist business.

It is fair to say that through the decade of the 1880s the Surf Hotel never suffered from lack of guests. The newer resort hotels were closer to New York and took less time to reach from the city, but even those that were built on the Atlantic Ocean beach did not threaten the Surf. It had carved a special niche for itself. The reasons are threefold: its location, personal service and family character. The Surf on Fire Island beach near the Inlet was a full six miles away from the mainland across the widest point of the Great South Bay. Because of this location it got cool sea breezes from both the south and the north, and guests could swim in either the ocean or the bay. They could also fish for the favored blues in either the ocean or the bay thanks to the nearby Fire Island Inlet. No other hotel resort on the Atlantic beach could make these claims. This favorable location, although harder to reach from the city, was recognized again and again by the regular guests who talked about it to correspondents of the newspapers.

Second, David S. S. Sammis, the proprietor, was always on hand from June to September and treated his guests as personal houseguests. That was also mentioned often by them. Many of them became repeat guests summer after summer, and many came from distant parts of the country for a week or two at the Surf.

Last, it was a resort for families, and while it did not exclude singles, it did discourage day-trippers and those who would only spend a night before departing.

Who came to the Surf and where did they come from?

Chapter Six
GUESTS AT THE SURF HOTEL

On July 8, 1868, an article was reported in the *New York Times* from its special correspondent at the Surf Hotel on Fire Island. It described the resort becoming more popular year by year and rapidly filling up, with the most choice apartments already engaged for the season. It went on to tell of all the attractions for guests and the warm welcome given by Mr. Sammis with his smiling countenance. After telling of the ease of getting there from New York City (the South Side Railroad to Babylon was completed that very week), the article concluded the report by saying, "Among the guests here are John Jacob Astor and Charles A. Dana." No others were mentioned by name.

For the Surf to attract Astor and Dana to spend their Fourth of July holiday in 1868 at its premises was indeed a huge coup. Not since the first summer at the chowder house in 1856 when newspaperman James Gordon Bennett Sr. came to its opening did the hotel have such prominent guests.

The John Jacob Astor mentioned in the *Times* article was actually the third of that name, the grandson of the J.J. Astor who came to the United States in 1784 at the age of twenty-one and made a fortune in fur trading, shipping, and New York City real estate. When he died in 1848 his estate was worth over $20 million, the largest in America up to that time. Much of this enormous wealth was passed on to his son, William Backhouse Astor, who, continuing to invest in the real estate of booming New York City, added greatly to the fortune. William retired in 1866, turning over the family business to his eldest son John Jacob Astor III, who had become the principal inheritor of his grandfather's wealth at the time of his death.* He became the titular head of the family, by far the richest person in America at the time of his visit to the Surf Hotel in 1868. He was also known as "a gentleman of leisure."[48]

Born in 1822, the third J.J. Astor graduated from Columbia College and studied at Göttigen, Germany's most prominent center of learning. Returning home, he married Augusta Gibbs and in 1848, the same year his grandfather died, they had a son, their only child, whom they named William Waldorf Astor, Walldorf being the name of the town in Germany where the immigrant Astor had been born.

John Jacob Astor III, as head of the family, played a prominent role in New York City life. In 1860 he was on the committee of five that welcomed the nineteen-year-old Albert, Prince of Wales, to New York and arranged a ball in honor of the heir to the English throne. Unlike many prominent New Yorkers in 1860, John was a Republican who actively supported Abraham Lincoln for president. (Lincoln, in winning the election, did not receive a majority of New York City votes; he did win the vote in the entire state, however.) Astor not only supported Lincoln but he supported the Union cause in ways that none of his peers did. At the age of thirty-nine he enlisted in the Union Army (most of his peers paid $300 for a replacement when the draft was instituted in 1863) and donated $3,000 of his own money to arm the tugboat *Yankee*. Later in the war General George McClellan of the Army of the Potomac appointed him his aide-de-camp. Astor rented a house in Washington complete with butler, valet and cook to properly serve McClellan. He moved south with the army to lay siege to Richmond. His commitment to the Union cause created great tension in his own family. His father William B. Astor was so opposed to the war that he refused to pay

---

* John Jacob Astor at his death in 1848 left one half of his estate to his favorite grandson JJA III in trust until the time of his own son William B. Astor's death. At that time in 1875, JJA III also received $20 million from his father. JJA III, the glint in grandfather Astor's eye, was thus given special consideration in the family and was the principal inheritor. There were no taxes on inherited wealth.

income taxes that were instituted to help finance it. He took his case to the Supreme Court and won it. There were no income taxes again until 1913.

It is likely that John Jacob Astor III came to the Surf Hotel that July with his wife and possibly with his 20-year-old son, William Waldorf. The latter at the death of his father in 1890 was thought to be worth between $50 and $80 million. That year he and his family left his country for England for good. There, in due course, he became Lord Astor, the First Viscount of Cliveden, and started the English branch of that family.

It is certainly true in the Gilded Age that wealthy and socially prominent people followed each other to resorts such as Newport and Bar Harbor. So the visit of the John Jacob Astors to the Surf Hotel in 1868 could only mean that more would follow. Sammis must have been very pleased.

Along with Astor on that Fourth of July weekend in 1868 was newspaper editor Charles A. Dana. A contemporary in age, Dana had started his career in 1847 at the *New York Tribune* under the guidance of the legendary Horace Greeley, first as his assistant and later as his managing editor. He was a great success but always wanted a paper of his own. At the time of his visit to the Surf Hotel he had just completed the purchase of the *New York Sun* and had become the chief editor of that old paper. Dana would become noted for his independent political views and his opposition to the labor movement. He made the *Sun* an influential newspaper, emphasizing colorful stories with eye-catching headlines, later carried to an extreme by W.R. Hearst in the *New York Morning Journal* and Joseph Pulitzer in the *New York World*.

Along with James Gordon Bennett's *New York Herald*, the *New York Sun* would also write about the Surf; by 1870 most New York and Brooklyn papers were sending correspondents at least once or twice a summer to cover special weekend events.

After the 1870 expansion the *New York Times* again sent a special correspondent to Fire Island to report on the larger establishment Sammis had created the previous winter. Again it received a favorable review, but what surprised and pleased him most was the weather. "Fire Island is the coolest place, with the exception of Tip Top House on Mount Washington, to be found east of the Mississippi River." He reported, "A select class of people on the hotel register who are now here or who have engaged rooms for the season include: William E. Dodge and family; Judge Anthony, William Thompson, and George Sterling, all of Poughkeepsie, New York; Jay Cooke and Thomas Hitchcock of New York; Fred Townsend of Albany (a cottage was named for him); Mr. Willoughby of Saratoga: Harvey Barnard of Utica; John M. Francis and H.T. Casswell of Troy; Mrs. Ireland and J.W. Schermerhorn of New York; Maturin Livingston Delafield of Riverdale; and Colonel and Mrs. Kinney of Washington D.C."[49]

For the first time we read of guests from outside New York City, including towns along the Hudson River—especially Albany, the state capital—as well as Washington D.C. After New York City, Albany would grow to be the second largest home of Surf Hotel guests, and the largest cottage would be named Albany Cottage. Fred Townsend from Albany would remain a guest for many years to come.

Some comments about a few of the above guests: Jay Cooke, a contemporary of Astor and Dana, was a financier whose firm Jay Cooke and Company played a large part in selling U.S. Government bonds during the Civil War. Afterwards he would finance railroad bonds during their huge expansion in the early 1870s. However, the firm became overextended and collapsed in September 1873, thereby precipitating the Great Panic of that year and the subsequent years of depression. When Cooke visited the Surf he was still riding the crest of the wave (figuratively of course).

Thomas Hitchcock was another prominent New York financier whose son would become America's greatest polo player in the 1920s. He was the Babe Ruth of that sport.

J.W. Schermerhorn was from an old New Amsterdam family that arrived in 1636. They became wealthy in the early nineteenth century at the same time Astor and many other merchants did. His sister Ann married Charles Suydam and his sister Catherine married Benjamin S. Welles. Both couples summered in Sayville and Islip along the Great South Bay. His other sister, Caroline, married William B. Astor Jr. (the younger brother of John Jacob Astor III mentioned above) and went on to become the acknowledged leader of New York Society during the peak of the Gilded Age. With wealth and old-family social pretensions, the Schermerhorns were also connected by marriage to the family of Frederic Jones, the father of Edith Wharton, the social novelist. The Frederic Jones family were Surf Hotel guests in June 1874.

Another old family that was a frequent guest at the Surf Hotel was the Livingston clan of the Hudson River Valley in New York. Their ancestor Robert Livingston, the son of a Scottish clergyman, had landed in Charlestown, Massachusetts, in December 1673 at the age of nineteen. Finding the religious orthodoxy there too similar to the Scottish, he quickly moved to Albany, New York, which was a growing town and very Dutch like its founders. Its most prominent Dutch citizen was Nicholas Van Rensselaer who had married Alida Schuyler of another prominent Dutch family. Because he could speak their language, Livingston fit in well with the patroons who controlled the land. Not long after his arrival, Van Rensselaer died and Livingston married his wife Alida, which set off a five-year battle for his estate. Mounting a vigorous campaign with the help of his wife, Livingston overcame all the legal obstacles and in July 1686 at the age of thirty-two was granted the patent for 160,000 acres of land in the east bank of the river, which became known as Livingston Manor. This was only the beginning. Later through marriage with the Beekman family, the Livingston clan gained control of 240,000 acres more. It is said that the family owned or controlled almost a million acres on both sides of the river in the upper Hudson Valley by the end of the second generation— a landed aristocracy. Robert also founded an American dynasty that included marriages to Schuylers, Beekmans, DePeysters, and Astors. Eventually Livingstons would marry their Livingston cousins. Many of these would play important roles in American history.

Maturin Livingston Delafield was a Surf Hotel guest in 1870. From his mother, the daughter of a Livingston who had married a Livingston cousin, Maturin would later inherit Montgomery Place, one of those gems considered the grandest of all the nineteenth-century Livingston estates. It has been restored and is open to the public today in Annandale, north of Rhinebeck, on the east bank of the river. Maturin was a cousin of John Jacob Astor III (mentioned above), both being descended from Robert R. Livingston, "the Judge" grandson of the founder, who married Margaret Beekman.

Four other Livingston families were recorded as Surf visitors in the decade of the 1870s. They were W. L. Livingston from New York in 1875; Johnston Livingston from Tivoli, also in 1875 and again in 1880; Edward Livingston of New York in 1880 and a cottage holder in 1882; and Mrs. Maturin S. Livingston of New York in 1880. Of these four, Johnston worked for his cousin William for a time in Philadelphia in the express freight business before moving back to the Hudson Valley where he occupied the family's manor in Tivoli called Sunning Hill and married his cousin Sylvie. Later, he would become a Patriarch, one of Mrs. Astor's group of 400 "friends" that would fit into her New York City ballroom.

The Maturin Livingstons lived in their manor home in Staatsburgh, New York, another grand Livingston estate somewhat south of the others but also on the east bank of the Hudson. They were both descended from the founder and thus cousins, although not close ones.

It was apparent by the end of the 1870s that the Surf Hotel had become a major attraction for families from the Hudson River Valley. The Livingston clan was the most prominent, but there were many others. There was a sizable group from the state capital, Albany. Adjutant General Fred Townsend (already mentioned) was joined by Erastus Corning (perennial mayor and political power in New York State), Philip Ten Eyck and Rufus King. King was the namesake and grandson of the Revolutionary War patriot from Massachusetts who moved to New York to become its first United States Senator (1789), twice a minister to Great

Britain and a candidate for the presidency. Judge Peckham from Albany had a distinguished legal career as a district attorney, a trial judge, and judge of the New York State Court of Appeals, the highest in the state, for a decade. In 1895 he would be nominated by President Grover Cleveland to the United States Supreme Court, where he served to his death in 1909. This group would keep Albany Cottage filled with lively political discussion.

Other Hudson River towns were represented on the guest list such as Poughkeepsie, Saugerties, Troy and Saratoga. From Mohawk Valley towns of Utica, Elmira, Waterford, Rochester and Buffalo many came for a summertime holiday on the beach. As word of the Surf grew, the geographic circle widened: from the South came guests from Philadelphia, Washington D.C. and even Alabama; from the West visitors hailed from Cincinnati, Chicago, Sacramento and Colorado, whose Governor S.A. Elberts was on the register in August 1880.

Jay Gould's *New York World* reported on September 20, 1879,* "Among the recent arrivals at the Surf Hotel, Fire Island, are Mrs. General E. B. Custer...." Elizabeth Bacon Custer was the widow of General George Armstrong Custer, who died three years earlier in the famous "last stand" against the Sioux Indians at the Battle of Little Bighorn in Montana. He had become an American hero for that stand, and Elizabeth spent much of her life (she died in 1933 at the age of ninety) in defense of the general's actions as it became clear that the battle was also the Sioux's last stand for independent ownership of land in the West (they were soon confined to reservations). The term "Mrs. General," unusual today, identified Elizabeth with her famous deceased husband in a very direct way.

Another notable guest in July was listed simply as Mrs. Roosevelt from Hyde Park. This was Mrs. James Roosevelt, born Rebecca Howland, who had married James in 1853. They

---

* *The New York World* was purchased in 1883 by Joseph Pulitzer of St. Louis.

had a son, also named James, but generally called "Rosy" by family and friends. James Roosevelt was a cousin of Theodore Roosevelt Sr. (father of the president) and his brothers who had chosen the North Shore of Long Island in the Oyster Bay area for their country homes, except for Robert who settled in Sayville on the South Shore. James, however, was part of the Hudson Valley branch of the family, with a home in Hyde Park on the east bank of the river. He was both a lawyer and a financier.

In 1876, the year following her visit to the Surf Hotel, Mrs. Roosevelt died and was survived by her husband James and her son Rosy. Four years later, James, then fifty-two years old, married young Sara Delano; a son was born whom they named Franklin Delano Roosevelt.

Meanwhile Rosy Roosevelt, the future president's much older half brother, had married Helen Astor, the second daughter of Mr. and Mrs. William B. Astor, New York Society leaders. Rosy and his wife lived in Vienna and then in London, where he was the Secretary in the United States Embassies in those two cities.

In addition to Mrs. Roosevelt, other prominent New Yorkers included the Coudert brothers, lawyers whose firm specialized in serving foreign clients and was the U.S. Counsel for several foreign governments such as France, Italy and Spain.* A small cottage at the Surf was named the Coudert cottage. Also George H. Peabody, William B. Prentice, J.R. Whiting and Frederick C. Havemeyer III were listed on the hotel register. The latter was a cousin of Henry Havemeyer who built the "Armory" on Captree Island in 1879 (see Chapter Fourteen).

Notable from the world of the arts and literature was Horace Greeley, founder and editor of the *New York Tribune*, who was seen on his way through Babylon to the Surf Hotel in August 1872, the year he ran for President of the United

---

* Coudert Brothers opened an office in Paris in 1879. It was the first American law firm to open offices in London, Singapore and Moscow.

States and lost to General Grant. There was also William F. Wharton and family, the brother-in-law of the novelist Edith Wharton, the architect Charles C. Haight, and the author Herman Melville with his suffering wife. Haight was a guest in August 1880 at a time early in what would become a successful career as an architect. In 1884 William Bayard Cutting asked him to design a country house on his land in Great River, Long Island. Westbrook became the Cutting family home until 1949 and today is the Cutting Arboretum. Later Haight designed homes in New York City for the well-to-do, as well as buildings such as a chapel for the General Theological Seminary in Chelsea Square, New York, and a library for Yale University in New Haven, Connecticut.

Herman Melville came to the Surf Hotel because his wife Elizabeth suffered from "rose cold," as hay fever was then called. He was arguably its most notable literary guest, at least the one who spent the most time there. In 1872 in a letter to a relative, Elizabeth Shaw Melville, Herman's wife, inquired about Fire Island as a place to escape from the hay fever afflictions from which she suffered every August. She wondered "if it is easy of access, and if there are more private and less expensive houses than the Surf Hotel." She added that "she would like to go there for a relief of Hay Fever which [she would] have to undergo in August."[50] Elizabeth's query about the cost of a month's holiday at the Surf reflected the fact that at that time the family had almost no money and depended entirely on Melville's low-end job as a customs inspector in the Port of New York. His pay was $4 a day or $20 a week for the five days of work. It only barely kept his family alive and did not provide time for writing, except for the occasional poem. Melville applied for and got this job in 1866 after all the money had run out.

By the mid 1850s he had written the successful books *Typee* and *Omoo* as well as his masterpiece *Moby Dick* (1851), which was badly reviewed, sold poorly, and led his publishers to slash his advances. His earnings were rapidly declining when he impulsively acquired a farm in the Berkshires with two mortgages, the payment on one of which he was

not able to make. By then he had become entirely depend-
ent on his wealthy father-in-law, Mr. Shaw, for support of his
large family. With a turn for the worse in the prospects for
the sale of his books, his health suffered as well. His move
to New York and the political job of customs inspector followed in 1866. He was forty-seven years old, his literary
career seemed over, and the title *Moby Dick* was only known
to a very few literary historians. Not even his few poems of
this era were published.

From 1866 to 1885, almost twenty years, Melville held
the daily job of customs inspector in New York. Tragedy came
to his family in the suicide of their eldest son, the second son's
emergence as a ne'er-do-well, and their daughter Bessie's
crippling rheumatism. It was during this time that Elizabeth
Melville inquired about Fire Island.

It is not clear when the first Melville visit to the Surf
Hotel took place, but in the year (1885) when Herman gave
up the customs inspector's job Elizabeth wrote to her cousin
from the Surf. "Herman came down on Friday and staid [sic]
till Monday morning, and seemed to enjoy it very much—I
am sure it will benefit him."[51] It is possible that they had visited before that year. A Boston paper noted that Melville was
staying at Fire Island in 1887, and it is likely that several
visits were made by the couple from 1885 to the author's
death in 1891. This was all made financially possible because
Elizabeth Melville had inherited a fortune at the death of
her father.

During those last few years of his life Melville wrote the
novel *Billy Budd*, probably much of it at the Surf Hotel, as
he often said writing was difficult for him in the city. Found
after his death in his desk drawer, it was not published until
1924. By then his reputation was on the rise, as *Moby Dick*
was being then hailed by some as an American classic.

There were prominent political figures who came to the
Surf Hotel for a holiday. Most notable of these were three
presidents of the United States, James A. Garfield, Chester
A. Arthur and Grover Cleveland. Garfield visited during the
time he was a Republican Representative in Congress before

being elected president in 1880. After his assassination in 1881 his successor Chester A. Arthur, a New York Republican, came to the Surf in the summer of 1883 after his visit to the "Armory" (see Chapter Fourteen). Finally Grover Cleveland with his political associates Daniel Lamont and Daniel Manning visited briefly during his campaign in the summer of 1888 while touring Long Island. Cleveland lost that election but regained the White House four years later. A Democrat, he had been raised in upstate New York, and had been mayor of Buffalo and Governor of New York before becoming president.

Two more very prominent New York political figures were Peter Cooper and Samuel J. Tilden. Tilden, very much like Grover Cleveland, was raised upstate, became a lawyer who was active in Democratic Party politics, and eventually was elected Governor of New York. Like Cleveland, he ran for president as a Democrat, but unlike him he failed to get a majority vote of the Electoral College in 1876 and thus lost in spite of gaining a popular majority. Probably Tilden's greatest achievement in politics was leading the effort that successfully ended the political life of Tammany boss William Marcy Tweed in New York City in 1874.

If any New Yorker was entitled to be listed as the leader of his city in the nineteenth century, Peter Cooper would have to be very close to the top of that list. A renaissance man in an industrial age, he was called an inventor, a manufacturer, an entrepreneur and a philanthropist. He was also deeply involved in the political life of his city and in 1876, at the great age of eighty-five, ran for president of the United States in the Greenback Party against the much younger Samuel J. Tilden. He finished the race in third place.

The guests at the Surf Hotel during the twenty-five years or so after the Civil War ended came from all walks of life, from all professions, and from many different locales. It was a remarkable story, a quiet retreat for most of them but with enough activities to keep boredom away. Almost all mentioned the friendly reception by David Sammis, who seemed to have been endowed with the perfect touch as host—warm, open, and lively, without ever being pushy or domineering. He knew what his guests wanted and they came back time and time again. It seemed like the Surf would go on and on in the summer of 1892. Sammis was seventy-four years old but was in good health and spirits. The nation's economy was healthy as well. No one could have predicted what was soon to transpire.

Chapter Seven

THE PARTITION OF FIRE ISLAND

In the 1870s an attempt was made to establish the legal ownership of land on Fire Island, which had been in question
since 1789. This became necessary because as the land was
seen to be more valuable after Sammis established a successful commercial enterprise, more disputes arose as to who
actually owned Fire Island.

To start in the seventeenth century when the English
first came to Long Island, the original grant of Fire Island
and the Great South Bay was made in 1693 by the English
Crown to Colonel William "Tangier" Smith. Smith had been
born in 1655 in Northhamptonshire, England, of a family
loyal to Charles, the king-in-exile at that time. After his
restoration and as a reward for their loyalty, the king in 1675
appointed William Smith the Lord Mayor of the Royal City
of Tangier in Morocco, an outpost opposite the Rock of Gibraltar
that had been given to England by Portugal as a dowry upon
Charles II's marriage to Catherine of Braganza (1662). From
that time forth Smith was known as William Tangier Smith.
In 1683 the English were forced to abandon Tangier, being
beset upon by Moors and Algerian pirates, and evacuated
Smith and other English people back home. He was said to
have lost a fortune at that time, which Charles II promised
to make good. Three years later, in 1686, the Smith family
sailed for Long Island where Colonel Smith was granted title
to about 40,000 acres of land. This patent covered mostly the
mainland, but also was on "the beach, meadow, and bay from
Huntington East Gut to a stake at Coptwange, the westernmost bounds of Southhampton on the beach running a distance east and west of twenty-four miles and seven chains."[52]

Smith called the colossal estate "The Manor of St. George." In 1705 he died in the manor house he had built at the eastern end of the Great South Bay in today's Mastic. It still stands as a museum open to the public. In his will he left the western portion of his beach property to his oldest son, Henry Smith, and the eastern portion to sons William and Charles. The dividing point was at Long Cove (near Watch Hill today). Henry Smith thus inherited all the beach from that point west to the inlet, which then was at Point O'Woods (but would change as the beach moved). For almost a century the inlet moved west to where the lighthouse is today, adding substantially to Henry Smith's legacy.

In 1789, several generations later, his descendant, also named Henry Smith, sold the beach land for two hundred pounds to "twenty yeomen of Brookhaven" who held it in common, each with an equal share to be used to graze cattle.[53] By then the inlet had moved further west to near where the lighthouse would be built, increasing the beach land to about twelve miles. This Henry Smith had grown up in Nova Scotia, where his father had lived as a Tory during the Revolution, and did not have any interest in holding vacant property on Long Island.

Over the following years it became unclear who the heirs of the twenty yeomen were and thus who owned this common land. Records were badly kept or lost. By 1855, when Sammis acquired his leases of 120 acres to build the Surf Hotel, he was not sure that the lessors owned the land he leased. Each of the proprietors retained the right to graze cattle and surely not all the descendents of the twenty yeomen of the common land agreed to the Sammis lease. He did have some conflicts with cattle grazers.

In 1871 Samuel W. Green, the owner of one-eighth of one share of the total property, sued Sammis, asking the court to partition the twelve miles by agreement or by auction. The court appointed a retired district attorney, Mr. Tuthill of Riverhead, to research the questions of title and to make a recommendation as to the partition of the land. This process would take seven years. Finally on January 18, 1878, Mr. Tuthill made his report to the court recommending that the beach from Long Cove (Watch Hill today) west to the Lighthouse be divided by partition in seventy-eight parcels, and "that the property can be partitioned amicably by Commissioners without fear of injury or loss to shareholders."⁵⁴

A surveyor had prepared a map entitled "Map of the Partition of the Great South Beach in the Towns of Brookhaven and Islip." David Sammis received the first lot on which the Surf Hotel stood and shared the second lot with Benjamin Sire, the co-owner of Dominy House. The referee recognized the value added to the lots by improvements that had been built on them. There were only three of these: the buildings and walks of the Surf Hotel at $80,000, together with eleven cottages at $12,000 to Mr. Sammis; a boarding house called Dominy House at $5,000 to Benjamin Sire; and two fish factories at $6,200 and $7,050 to Smith and Yarrington and the South Bay Oil and Guano Company. Smith and Yarrington were co-partners of the latter company. All ended up owning land they had originally leased because of the improvements they had made on it.

In addition to the above, only thirty individuals were identified as descendants of the twenty yeomen of 1789 and were awarded lots. The Town of Islip received no lots at all, and only a small portion of land was not divided nor awarded. All of the ownership of Fire Island Beach today, from the Lighthouse east to Long Cove, comes from that awarded in the partition of 1878. No one else at that time put forward a claim, and later claims were consistently denied by courts as not being brought in time.

Chapter Eight

THE FISH FACTORIES AND THE FISHING PIER

In addition to the two hotels—The Surf Hotel and Dominy House—the only other commercial buildings on Fire Island in 1878 were two fish factories; one belonging to the South Bay Oil and Guano Company, located east of the Point O'Woods, and Gil Smith's at Seaview. A third was built in 1880 near Smith Point to the east.

After 1850, a commercial industry developed on Long Island to process menhaden—or bunkers as they were generally known—by steaming the fish to extract their oil, which was used to make paint, to tan leather, and to add to the more expensive cod liver oil. The remains were ground up for fertilizer (guano). These factories were first built on the mainland, but the odor was so horrific that communities would not long tolerate them, and they moved to Fire Island. The industry was profitable for a time and fish factories were seen on the south beach all the way to Montauk Point. However by 1900 they were outdated. Two of these on Fire Island burned down, some thought by arson. Gil Smith's in Seaview, the last one, burned in 1910.

Another form of commercial fishing began in the 1880s in the area of today's Lonelyville where Captain Selah Clock of the Islip family built a four-hundred-foot pier into the ocean and established the Fire Island Fishing Company. At that time piers were being built far out into the ocean at Coney Island, Brighton Beach, and others were planned at Long Beach. These were for amusement parks and recreation. However Clock's pier was for commercial use—to shorten the time and avoid the hazard for fishing boats going through the often treacherous Fire Island Inlet. A rail track was laid from the ocean end of the pier, where fishing boats were unloaded of their catch, across the sand and out some distance into the bay. There the cargo was unloaded onto a bay boat for shipment to Islip or other mainland docks. A 1,600-foot fishing net also extended into the ocean from the pier head, which was hauled daily and emptied, adding to the transport across Great South Bay. The ocean pier lasted long after the rail track passed into history and was replaced by summerhouses. It was not repaired and was completely destroyed by the 1938 hurricane.

Chapter Nine
THE LIFE-SAVING STATIONS

Except for the occasional temporary fisherman's shacks, the only buildings on Fire Island in 1880 were the lighthouse with its keeper's house, the Surf Hotel complex, the Dominy House, the fish factories, the two telegraph towers, and the U.S. Life-Saving Stations. The latter were located on the beach from east to west at Smith's Point, Bellport, Blue Point, Lone Hill, Point O'Woods, and Fire Island somewhat west of the lighthouse. Two more were at Oak Island Beach and Gilgo Beach, both west of the Inlet. There were also some houses of refuge between these fully manned and equipped stations.

The United States Life-Saving Service was organized in 1871 to replace the Life-Saving Benevolent Association of 1849, a philanthropic institution with a voluntary staff that was ineffective and did not save many lives. In the face of many tragedies from lives lost in shipwrecks along the Great South Beach, the U.S. Congress funded the new federal service and appointed Sumner I. Kimball to organize a team of men who would be highly trained for the dangerous work of life-saving and would be paid for that work. The standards developed for the work were high and the conditions in which they lived and worked were made as comfortable as could be expected on the beaches of Long Island.

The life-saving stations were built to withstand severe storms and could be moved when erosion threatened. Each station consisted of four rooms on the ground floor, a boat room, a mess, a storeroom, and a keeper's room. On the upper floor were two dormitories, one for the crew of six men and another for shipwreck survivors who could not be immediately evacuated to the mainland. On top of the station was a lookout that was manned in daylight hours. Most challenging were the night patrols along the beach from station to station three miles or so apart, spent watching and listening for ships in distress and for cries of help. When a wreck was sighted or heard, all stations on the beach and the mainland were alerted by a telegraph line, which was installed in 1873 by Western Union, from Smith's Point all the way to the Surf Hotel. The Oak Island Beach Station exists today and is used by the residents as a community center.

The lifeboats themselves were shaped like the dories of the Grand Banks cod fishermen. Sturdy and well equipped, they were built of cedar planks over all-oak frames, twenty-five to twenty-seven feet long, seven feet wide with a shallow draft of only six to seven inches. They were always painted white for maximum visibility at sea and could be rowed by the six crewmen with long oars and guided by the keeper in the stern with a tiller on the rudder or a steering oar. They were very sea worthy and managed heavy surf efficiently and safely. Very seldom did they ever capsize, either going out through the surf or returning, which often was more the difficult task.

In addition to a life boat, each station was fully equipped with the "Lyle Gun" (a brass cannon for firing a projectile with a line attached to a ship in distress), a life car, a breeches buoy and other needed essentials for rescuing people off ships wrecked sometimes quite far out on a bar.

In the beginning the Fire Island stations were manned only in the winter months from November to April, when most wrecks occurred. Soon, however, that period was increased to ten months—July and August were for vacation during which the men were not paid. By 1890, a seventh man was added to the crew, making a total of sixty-four men for the eight Fire Island stations.

The United States Life-Saving Service made a huge contribution to reducing shipwreck deaths along the Long Island Great South Beach. From 1871 until 1915, when it was merged into the Coast Guard Service, it was a vital part of life there. By the advent of the twentieth century most vessels were steam driven and equipped with radio communication so that wrecks were much less frequent.

Chapter Ten

THE GREAT CHOLERA SCARE
THE SURF HOTEL 1892 AND
AFTERWARDS

By 1892 the Surf Hotel was starting to show its age. It had been over twenty years since David Sammis had expanded the premises by adding a new wing to the main building and an annex and eleven cottages. The original structure was thirty-five years old. The sun, sand and salt water had taken their toll, and guests were beginning to notice some ramshackle conditions in the resort. Furthermore, Sammis himself was seventy-four years old that summer and perhaps he also was tiring of spending every summer as its welcoming host. He only had one son, Joseph, of his second marriage, who was thirty-three that summer but did not have the outgoing personality of his father. It was very clear by then that the old man wanted top dollar for his lifetime effort and the large amount of investment he had put into the hotel.

In 1890 "a syndicate of New York capitalists" made Sammis an offer of $125,000 for the entire hotel property. He replied, "My price is $150,000, not a penny less,"[55] and negotiations were suspended for the year. However the following summer the syndicate returned with a new offer of $140,000, a $15,000 increase over that of the previous year. Sammis did not budge. Although the local press thought a compromise would be reached before 1892 and the Surf would be in new hands, it was not. The hotel business was booming then and Sammis would wait for his price to be met. There was much speculation about who the capitalists were. It was said they had ten million dollars to invest and that the group included a Belmont, but that was never confirmed. As it turned out, business booked for 1892 was so good that Sammis's price rose sharply.

Over the popular Fourth of July weekend many of the regular guests returned and were greeted by Sammis as usual in his warm and welcoming way. The prosperity of the 1880s had continued and the country watched to see if former President Grover Cleveland, who had once been a guest at the hotel, would defeat President Benjamin Harrison and serve a second term in office, one apart from his first. (He did). It was a good summer for Sammis and the Surf. On Labor Day the *New York Times* reported that 175 guests had arrived for the weekend from New York, White Plains, Yonkers and Brooklyn. There had often been a larger Labor Day crowd, but this was not an insignificant number. Sammis had every reason to believe that his property was not declining in value. There was, however, a dark cloud far away in the distance over the horizon that no one at the Surf could see, and no one that summer could possibly have imagined would ever come near that pleasant spot on Fire Island Beach.

In July and early August there was very occasional mention in the back pages of the New York daily papers that in Russia an epidemic of cholera, which had started in Persia (Iran today), had taken hold and was devastating the population. This was so far away that no one in the United States paid any attention at all, not even the health authorities. It could only spread across the ocean by traveling in ships, and very few if any came to New York from Russia. But that dark cloud did move to the cities of Europe, particularly to the German city of Hamburg where many Russian and Polish refugees had come fleeing the Czar. New York began to take notice, for in Hamburg there was a large fleet of ships of the Hamburg-American Lines that traveled the Hamburg to New York route, the larger ships stopping at Southampton, England, to take on more passengers. On all these ships the steerage passengers were almost entirely emigrants very tightly packed together, never being allowed to come up to mix with the transient cabin class. German and Polish immigration was at peak levels in the USA in 1892, many immigrants being of Jewish origin.

In August, a number of Russian Jews arrived in Hamburg to take passage for New York on the ship *Moravia* of the Hamburg-American Lines, due to sail on August 17. They were among 385 steerage passengers who had been given a clean bill of health from the American consul who certified that when the ship sailed there were no infections or contagious diseases prevalent in Hamburg. It turned out that he had been deceived by the authorities, who were trying to protect their city from panic. In fact, the plague had become an epidemic, and some of the Russian passengers were carriers of cholera.

On August 23, while *Moravia* was crossing the ocean, the American consul in Hamburg alerted New York health authorities of the contagion, to prepare them for the quarantine that would likely be required. Dr. William T. Jenkins, chief officer of the New York State Commission on Health, was in charge of planning for a pending epidemic with little time to spare. By the end of the month of August four ships were due to arrive in the Port of New York from Hamburg. It seems that Dr. Jenkins did a competent job of planning for the sick and the dead. A temporary hospital in tents was set up on Hoffman Island in the Lower Bay and a morgue established on nearby Swinburne Island. However, little attention was given to what would be done with healthy passengers who would have to be quarantined, especially those in the cabin class. On five ships there would be several hundred of them who could not be left aboard for any length of time without adequate provisions.

On the evening of August 30, *Moravia* arrived in the Lower Bay at the Quarantine Station and was boarded the next morning by the health officer. The ship surgeon reported that the boat had a clean bill of health and was anxious to get to dock in Hoboken. Upon further check of the written report however, it turned out that there had been twenty-four cases of cholera aboard and twenty-two had died during the voyage. *Moravia* was ordered to quarantine near Sandy Hook,

New Jersey, and would remain there for twenty days upon order of President Harrison on September 1, 1892. *Moravia* would be the first of five ships from Hamburg so ordered over the next ten days, all of which had cases of cholera aboard, deaths at sea as well as deaths in the port of New York. The last ship of the five to arrive from Hamburg on September 10, *Scandia*, was the worst infected ship of all. She had sailed on August 28 when the epidemic was raging in the stricken city with as many as 2,500 deaths a day.* On board were twenty-eight cabin and 981 steerage passengers. On the voyage there were thirty-two deaths. Seven were ill upon arrival and taken to nearby Swinburne Island. That same day two more died and two more were taken ill, one of whom died, making a total of thirty-five deaths of *Scandia* passengers. The total deaths in the five ships came to eighty-five.

A cholera epidemic was not a new experience for New York in the nineteenth century. There had been plagues in 1832, 1849 and 1852. In fact, in 1866 it was reported that 200 deaths per thousand occurred in the worst wards of the city from diseases including cholera on a regular basis. By the 1890s, however, led by the reformer Jacob Riis, the city made great strides in cleaning up the filth in the streets and repairing the leaking sewer system that had provided a breeding ground for rats that spread cholera. And the city health department under the direction of Dr. Hermann Biggs imposed a rigorous quarantine on ships from Europe when notified of diseases aboard. When all of the ships had been cleared to land, and the threat was over at the end of September, only nine people who lived in New York had died from cholera. An epidemic had been prevented. But what of all the passengers on the five ships who had remained healthy? Here the record was not good.

---

* During the height of the epidemic in Hamburg the *New York Herald* reported daily, usually on the front page, in both English and German, an account of the tragedy. The paper was read by thousands of German immigrants living in Manhattan and Brooklyn who had arrived in the past twenty years and who did not read the English language.

It was not until September 7, eight days after the arrival of *Moravia*, that the U.S. Government offered Dr. Jenkins the reservation on Sandy Hook called Camp Low, for the healthy passengers on *Moravia* and the much larger *Normannia* which had arrived from Hamburg via Southampton, England, on September 3 with about 600 cabin and 500 steerage passengers. On the latter ship, crew and passengers were being stricken while she was anchored in quarantine; the disease was actively spreading and the danger of panic was great. It seemed imperative to get healthy people off by keeping them in quarantine ashore for the twenty days. Dr. Jenkins did not favor Sandy Hook, as the facilities were not adequate for so many people and barracks had to be built.* His choice was the Surf Hotel on Fire Island, which could handle all 600 cabin passengers from *Normannia*.

On September 9, David Sammis went to New York City to meet with a representative of Dr. Jenkins about the sale of the Surf Hotel to the State of New York. He was told that Governor Roswell P. Flower would pay him $150,000 for all of the hotel property, the same amount that he had asked the syndicate the year before. The hotel would immediately be used to house the 600 *Normania* passengers for the duration of the quarantine. Sammis considered this offer overnight and the next morning replied that he would accept nothing less than $225,000! Knowing that the passengers were already aboard the small steamer *Stonington*, he had increased his asking price by fifty percent. The State of New York was at his mercy and he knew it. Finally, as a "generous act" he agreed to sell for $210,000 on the condition the governor pay $50,000 in cash immediately and the balance in six months time. The governor was forced to agree and sent his personal, certified check for the down payment and accepted responsibility for the balance.

By nightfall on September 10, the Surf Hotel belonged to the State of New York. All the guests soon departed and the

---

* Barracks were built on Sandy Hook for healthy passengers of the other ships at the expense of Austin Corbin, President of the Long Island Railroad.

staff was ready for 600 new ones. However *Stonington* had not arrived and the local community was making sure that no passengers from any cholera ship would ever come to Fire Island. A small but fierce rebellion was underway against the State of New York and its governor, and Sammis quickly became the most hated man in Babylon. When he finally left the Surf, a writer wrote, "We chanced to walk down the dock with Mr. Sammis as he left his famous old hostelry he had built and for thirty-seven years conducted. As he left the doorway he turned squarely about and facing the hotel, raised his hat and said, 'Good-bye, Fire Island.' It was really an impressive moment and we shall always remember the occurrence."[56] When he reached Babylon, he quickly retreated to New York until local anger had cooled.

Meanwhile the 600 *Normannia* passengers were undergoing a trial of their own. During the afternoon of September 10 they had boarded the steamboat *Stonington* for passage to the Surf Hotel on Fire Island. *Stonington* had been purchased by the financier J. Pierpont Morgan for this very purpose—an act of generosity on his part—but she was an old boat and was delayed in arriving at the side of *Normannia* by bad weather. Further delay was caused since each passenger was examined by a doctor before boarding. Finally at 6:00 P.M. when all was ready the captain decided it was too late to get to Fire Island Inlet before dark and that they would lay over for the night in the protection of Sandy Hook. By morning the wind had freshened from the southeast and the captain refused to make the passage as it would not be safe, he felt, for the 600 persons on his boat. Only then was the Iron Steamboat Company's boat *Cepheus* chartered to make the trip. *Cepheus*, named after the constellation, was seaworthy, but was designed as a day boat for no more than 400 passengers. She did not have any sleeping accommodations but did have a kitchen of sorts.

While the authorities were struggling with the problem of getting 600 healthy passengers to the Surf Hotel on September 11, not a small number of people in Babylon and Bay Shore were taking steps to see that they would never be able to safely land at the hotel dock. An act of rebellion was underway, supported by an injunction issued by a state judge. Many of the Great South Bay men (called clam diggers by the New York press), fearful that their livelihood was in jeopardy due to cholera and its effect on shellfish harvesting (an order of oysters had already been cancelled by a large New York oyster house), organized to oppose the landing of passengers at the Surf Hotel. Leadership of the group was taken by the Town of Islip Board of Health and Dr. William A. Baker, as well as the town supervisor (the Town of Islip included the villages from West Islip to Bayport). It was this group that requested Justice Barnard of the State Supreme Court sitting in Brooklyn to enjoin Governor Flower, Dr. Jenkins, David Sammis and captains of both *Stonington* and *Cepheus* from landing passengers at the Surf Hotel or anywhere else on Fire Island. Justice Barnard issued the order and scheduled a hearing for September 12 in the morning. In the meantime, the bay men, some of whom had been deputized, prepared to enforce the injunction and proceeded to Fire Island in their clam boats with their shotguns, threatening to burn down the hotel. They occupied the nearby Muncie Hotel and waited for the arrival of the steamboat *Cepheus*, which had been spotted off Point Lookout at the Jones Beach Inlet.

Governor Flower responded to these events by statements condemning the threats of the bay men, challenging the authority of the Islip Board of Health, and ordering units of the Sixty-Ninth Infantry Regiment to be shipped by steamboat to Fire Island. She carried 275 Naval Reserves and 260 men of the Sixty-Ninth. In addition, 428 militiamen of the Brooklyn Thirteenth Regiment (National Guard) were ordered to Babylon by the Long Island Railroad to keep the peace there. They were quartered at the bowling alleys and in other parts of the Watson House on Fire Island Avenue.

SEVENTY-TWO HOURS ON *CEPHEUS*

By 4:00 P.M. on September 11, *Cepheus* had proceeded alongside *Stonington* anchored off Sandy Hook, had loaded all its 600 passengers aboard, and had set forth for the Fire

Island Inlet, about three to four hours away. It was just possible to get there before dark. On board was Caspar W. Whitney, a correspondent for *Harper's Weekly*, assigned to cover what could have been an extraordinary event in American history*

The last and crowning series of blunders in the handling of these unhappy people began on Sunday afternoon, September 11. They had withstood the plague, sustained hunger and thirst, but insult was now to be added to injury.

They were hurried on board the *Cepheus* in the afternoon about two, and sent off to Fire Island. Every captain of any kind of craft knows that the Fire Island Inlet is one of the most difficult and dangerous on the Atlantic coast, and that it can only be navigated at high water, and with a pilot. Despite this well-known fact, and in the face of strenuous objections from both the captains of the *Cepheus* and *Stonington*, these people were sent off on rough five hours' trip, and with the certain knowledge that when the Inlet was reached they would probably be obliged to turn around and go back.

The wretched experiences of that trip are simply indescribable. The captain dared not attempt to cross the dangerous bar, and it was too rough to lay outside. There was nothing to do but to put back. And what a night it was! Six hundred people on an excursion steamer, no sleeping accommodations, nothing to eat, and all the women and children and half the men seasick. The decks were literally covered with those who, too sick to raise their heads, lay in their own vomitings. It was two o'clock the next morning when they finally reached the *Stonington*, and went back to their dirty quarters, to the sandwiches and coffee they had left many hours before, and to their bunks, from which a drunken and unrestrained crew had thrown their bedding. It was a fitting ending to a day of mental and physical torture.

Again, the next morning, September 12th, they were put on the *Cepheus*, and went back over the course on which they had spent so many miserable hours the day before, only once more to meet with disappointment at the end of the journey, this time keener because unexpected.

Lawyer Reid's mob of clam-diggers had possession of the wharf, and would not permit a landing, threatening

---

* *Harper's Weekly* was owned by the firm Harper and Brothers, a publisher of books. It was considered a politically oriented newspaper that started in 1857.

violence if such an attempt was made, and talking. Both Senator McPherson and R.M. Thompson argued long and earnestly with Reid, but the lawyer was not to be turned from his despicable course to keep these people off Fire Island. They then appealed to the mob, begging that the women, one or two of whom were about to become mothers, and the children, actually suffering from cold and hunger, might be allowed to land, but the mob only jeered them, shouting to them "go back to Europe," and jeering again over their brutal wit.

Islip ought to be proud of its pettifogging lawyer and the brutal mob of baymen that did his bidding. They hooted at the men on the *Cepheus*, who pleaded for bread for the women and children, and one wretch waved a loaf at them.

That night was another of suffering; 600 of them on an excursion boat large enough for 400, no sleeping accommodation, and one small oil stove. Hunger and cold kept most of them wide awake; and those who did rest were the older women and the children, to whom had been given a few mattresses sent from shore by the Quarantine doctor in charge. The next day—Tuesday September 13th—found their situation desperate; but relief was near at hand. On Monday the *Harper's Weekly* tug had been steaming about upper and lower Quarantine and Sandy Hook camp and on Tuesday started for Fire Island. It was dangerously rough at the Inlet, but no pilot would come to us, though I managed to buy the avaricious soul of the skipper of a fishing-smack, and we got in. As we steamed up, the mob on the wharf was visible, which the *Cepheus* lay off not over a hundred yards, with every one of her decks black with the *Normannia's* passengers. When we drew near, we saluted the exiles, and they cheered us in return. We told them the good news of the dissolution of the injunction and the militia being ordered out and again they cheered and cheered.

Then we steamed up to the wharf and to a fleet of cat-boats in which were Reid's clam-diggers. They had heard the news, and were beginning to make tracks homeward; they scattered in all directions, and in ten minutes not one remained in sight. Now the news of deliverance was given the passengers officially, and shortly afterwards the *Cepheus* yawl was put out with Senator McPherson, R.M. Thompson, A.M. Palmer, and Mr. Wall, the hotel manager; these were the first to land, and a shout from the boat greeted their first steps on terra firma. An hour afterwards the Cepheus came to the wharf with the assistance of the *Harper's Weekly* tug. As the gangplank was run up, the band began playing

"Hail Columbia" and the long-suffering passengers were delivered from durance vile.

What a pathetic and joyful scene it was! As the passengers came out of the boat, they formed a procession, marching up the long wharf to the hotel, some singing and laughing, many with tears running down their cheeks, all with drawn, anxious faces, the result of their terrible experience. I believe I could write half the paper on my observations and impressions. I had intended when I began this article to confine myself entirely to what I saw in my two days about the quarantined, but I became so interested in the subject of their treatment that I have made my observations the basis of a protest against such blundering management. This should be a lesson to the government never to be forgotten. If it will result in the proper facilities being afforded at quarantine, and the management thereof becoming Federal, the misery of the *Normannia's* first cabin passengers, among whom there was not a single case of sickness from first to last, will not leave so bitter a remembrance. Best of all, let there be a suspension of immigration.[57]

The deliverance referred to above was that on September 13, Justice Barnard's injunction was rapidly set aside by his colleagues after a short hearing on the matter of the Brooklyn Courthouse on the ground that he had no jurisdiction to issue it, nor did he have the authority to arrest Dr. Jenkins to prevent him from doing his duty as an officer of the State of New York. The authority of the state, its governor, and its officers was fully upheld by the Court. It was made clear that *Cepheus* should dock and discharge its passengers at the Surf Hotel and that Dr. Jenkins, who had gone to the hotel during the night by then, should do all he could to make their life comfortable.

When the bay men heard the news of the injunction being lifted, and that soldiers were coming, they quickly retreated to the mainland. That part of the crisis was over, at least for a time. That no one at the Surf was ill eased the feeling of panic that had spread all around the bay area.

Dr. Jenkins acted quickly. He obtained the governor's permission to release the 600 *Normannia* passengers and on September 16, just three days after their arrival at the Surf, the majority of them boarded *Cepheus* again for the trip back to dock in Hoboken where they had been scheduled to land on September 3. Their nightmare had lasted almost two weeks. The return voyage of *Cepheus* was not without incident. With all anxious to get to New York, three hours were lost on a sand bar off Oak Island where *Cepheus* had run aground because the tide was too low for her heavily loaded state. The passengers were angry and one shouted, "There is a Jonah aboard, we will never reach New York." But as the tide rose three hours later she pulled free, helped by Captain Weeks of the Fire Island Life-Saving Station. A few of the passengers chose to return by train from Babylon. There was a risk for them too, but with the soldiers still there they were not harmed. The troops remained on Fire Island since cholera ships were still arriving in New York and Dr. Jenkins might need the rooms at the Surf again.

Sure enough, almost as a coda to this whole tragic cholera epidemic, on September 18, "with flags flying the steamer *Cepheus* came over the treacherous bar of the inlet this after noon bearing the cabin passengers of the *Wyoming* who are to spend the balance of the week in the new quarantine. Among them were eighty-one first- and 204 second- cabin passengers. The Surf had some new late season guests.... The threatened invasion of baymen from the shore did not occur, and it has transpired that the service of the Islip Board of Health's order to vacate was only a formality."[58] However, just to be sure, seventy-eight men of the Thirteenth arrived the next day, making a complement of over 300 soldiers and thirty-five police to protect a small group of "guests." The bay men remained peaceful but the authorities were obviously edgy. The guests desperately wanted to get home, but were delayed because two children had come down with a disease, which was later determined to be typhoid fever, not cholera. This delayed their departure until September 23.

The Thirteenth Regiment also left on September 23, but was replaced by 250 soldiers of the Fourteenth and Forty-Seventh Regiments to protect the State's property. It was not until October 5th that parts of the hotel were closed for the winter and all the troops left for home. There had been a fear that local bay men might burn the place down so it could never be used as a quarantine again. That did not happen. However, on the south shore there continued to be bad feeling against the state's ownership of the Surf. In 1894 efforts were made by Suffolk County Supervisors to force the State to sell the property by legislative action and local political pressure. This did not work and state ownership continued.

The cholera epidemic died out in Europe and never affected the United States, thanks to the work of Dr. Jenkins and others. The papers reported "stamping out infections" on September 17; "there is no cholera in New York" on September 19, the day after *Wyoming* passengers went to the Surf Hotel; and "cholera no longer feared" on September 20, although two people died that day at Camp Low on Sandy Hook. On September 23, all ship passengers on *Moravia*, the first of the cholera ships, were released, as well as those on *Wyoming*. The efforts of New York health officials to mobilize against the epidemic kicked off pioneering city progress at preventive medicine against many other diseases as well, especially diphtheria and tuberculosis. The accounts in the New York papers had shown a positive ending to the crisis. That was not the case, however, in the Babylon paper.

The article in Babylon's *South Side Signal* described the events of September 11 to 13 in an entirely different light. The armed clam diggers of the *New York Herald* became peaceful bay men, protecting their source of work, the Great South Bay, from pollution and disease, who were within their rights to enforce the injunction of Justice Barnard to forbid a landing of *Cepheus*; and who departed when the injunction was vacated. It described Governor Flower calling out the troops "for reasons known only to himself" as an extreme overreaction. The crowd at the Surf Hotel dock while *Cepheus* attempted to land "was intensely interested and strongly opposed to the occupancy of the Surf Hotel by *Normannia's* passengers, but they were there as onlookers rather than as participants in the resistances... They were prepared to make proper resistance."[59] There was no mention of their being armed with shotguns (see photograph) or their casting off *Cepheus*'s lines, or of the two sheriff's deputies posted twenty-four hours a day at the Babylon Town dock to prevent anyone from Fire Island landing for any reason, even to secure food and medicine.

Henry Livingston, the publisher and editor of the *Signal* was more blunt in his editorial that day, entitled "Flower's Fiasco." "The people of Babylon," he said, " regardless of political preference, are a unit in denouncing the un-called-for and despotic action of Governor Flower in sending nearly 1000 armed men into a peaceful community for no reason whatever, except that he chose to accept as facts a mass of the most damaging fabrication sent out by an army of reporters, writing 'on space.'

"By sending the soldiers down here he has done the people of this part of the South Side an irreparable injury. The tidings of his action have been telegraphed to all parts of the country, and our people have been represented as an ignorant, vicious and lawless class, ripe for carnage, utterly lacking in the sense of decency, and in need of subjection by force of arms."[60]

Perhaps the Governor did order a larger force than was needed, and perhaps they stayed too long, But no injury occurred, except to pride, and no life was lost, nor did anyone contract cholera. Normality did come back to Fire Island, Babylon, and Bay Shore by the end of October when the Surf was closed up for the winter.

AFTER THE CHOLERA SCARE

It wasn't until May 9, 1893, almost eight months after the day Sammis and Dr. Jenkins struck a deal over the sale of the Surf Hotel that the former got all his money and New York took legal title to the property. May 9 that year was one day after Sammis's seventy-fifth birthday and his present from the taxpayers of New York amounted to $160,000 (the balance due after the $50,000 in cash he received the past September). There had been a lengthy title search, made complicated because at the time of the 1878 Partition of Fire

Island, not all claimants for land came forward or could be found (see Chapter Seven). The attorney who searched the title for the state, Mr. Jones, ran up a bill of over $6,000 for handling the matter, which was noted in the *New York Times* and was of concern to many state legislators. The six months mentioned in the contract passed and still the legislature did not act. Finally a court disqualified any late claimants for hotel and land, and the bill passed. The State of New York paid a total of $216,000 for the property that was likely worth less than half that amount in its then run-down condition. Many improvements were needed for it to open again as a resort for the public and it was too late to do that in 1893.

Furthermore, the climate in the country had abruptly changed for the worse that winter. Another panic occurred which was followed by the most severe economic crisis in U.S. history up to that time and by a five-year depression. Unlike the earlier panics, which had occurred about every twenty years, this one did not come as a sudden shock. It began in England in 1890 with the collapse of the financial house of Baring Brothers, but did not spread to the United States until February 1893 with the bankruptcy of the Philadelphia and Reading Railroad and then the National Cordage Company. By summer the credit system failed, stock prices plummeted, fortunes disappeared and 140 national and hundreds more state banks closed their doors. It was a major financial panic. By the end of 1893, 16,000 businesses had failed, a figure that included one-third of the railroads in the country. J.P. Morgan was hard at work reorganizing his many railroads.

During the depression that followed, unemployment rose to about twenty-percent of the workforce; civil strife broke out between companies and the unions; federal troops and state militias were out to battle miners and railroad workers. In New York City, layoffs reached high levels during the winter of 1893–94; twenty-thousand people were homeless as well as jobless. Anarchists such as Emma Goldman told the crowds that came to hear her that rather than petitioning the authorities, they should march by the homes of the wealthy and demand relief. "If you are hungry and need bread, go and get it. The shops are plentiful and the doors are open," she said.[61] Such militant words had not been heard in New York since the Civil War draft riots.

In this climate it was almost a miracle that the Surf Hotel would ever open again, but as the spring of 1894 arrived on Long Island, Charles A. Merritt became the lessee of the hotel. For many years he had managed the government hotels in Kingston, Jamaica. Charles I. Cunningham, formerly of Manhattan Beach and Brighton Beach hotels, became his manager. Substantial improvements were made by the state that spring and a June opening was planned. The financial arrangement provided "that the state would receive sixty-seven percent of the net receipts and retain the right to terminate the lease at any time the place may be required for quarantine emergency."[62] The state legislature had authorized the Department of Health to lease the property for hotel purposes, and Merritt took on that challenge.

Prior to opening in June 27, a group from Albany including Dr. Jenkins, who was still the state health commissioner, attended a lunch at the Surf, examined the premises, and evidently were pleased with what they saw. Dr. Jenkins' health was toasted at lunch, and he said he was pleased to be back under much happier circumstances.

Many of the old-timers returned to the resort for the July 4 weekend. Those well known in New York and Brooklyn were the majority, but other cities also were represented. One name on the register was familiar to everyone: D.S.S. Sammis and family. It does seem strange that the seventy-six-year-old Sammis would return again for what would be a final visit that summer. Perhaps he could not stay away, having been there for every summer since 1856 except the past one when the hotel was not open. His health had been failing and he knew the end was not far off.

The summer was a successful one. In late July the manager entertained with a full-dress hop, the first of the season. There were guests from Indianapolis and Chicago that weekend, as well as many from Bay Shore, Babylon and vicinity. All the ugliness of September 1892 seemed to have disappeared. The hotel was beautifully decorated with bunting and Chinese lanterns.

Chapter Eleven
THE DEATH OF DAVID SAMMIS
1895

In the fall of 1894 after his last visit to the Surf Hotel, his first as a guest, Sammis was inflicted with kidney failure, known at that time as Bright's disease. He went south that winter hoping to regain his strength, but to no avail. He returned in a greatly weakened state to his house in Babylon and died there on May 18, 1895. He had just celebrated his seventy-seventh birthday. He left behind his very large family who lived in a house on East Main Street in the village: his second wife Antoinette Wheeler Sammis (his first wife had died in 1852 without having any children), a son Joseph, and five daughters: Louise, Antoinette, Sarah Elizabeth, Blanche and Madeleine. A sixth daughter, Annie, predeceased him. Sadly, his only son Joseph died on December 1, in the same year as his father.

Although building and successfully operating the Surf Hotel for almost forty years was Sammis's great accomplishment, he was also involved in a major way in Babylon, his home ever since he had left New York City to cast his lot in the area where he was born. He became a large owner of Babylon real estate, was interested in the local water and electric-light companies, and was one of the organizers of the Babylon National Bank. He controlled the weekly newspaper, the *Babylon Budget*, a rival of Henry Livingston's *South Side Signal*. He also built (in 1871) and operated the Babylon horse railroad (see Chapter Five). Politically a Republican, he was active in local and county politics. He was appointed Overseer of Highways of Babylon in 1882, a political appointment. He was also a member of a group known as the Islip

Driving Park Association, founded in 1881 to promote trotting and horse racing at a track in Islip north of the railroad tracks on Moffitt Boulevard. It was a popular sport in that era, and other members included his son Joseph Sammis, summer residents William K. Vanderbilt, Bradish Johnson, Edward S. Knapp, George Lorillard, Schuyler Parsons and August Belmont, as well as Ned Dominy, George Clock and other leading local citizens. It was a special distinction for Sammis to be included in this group of men.

In 1870, Sammis, with several other prominent Babylon men including "Uncle" Jesse Conklin, Henry Livingston (editor of the *South Side Signal*) and William R. Foster (an early Babylon summer resident), made a serious attempt to reorganize the governance of Babylon to that of an incorporated village with an elected mayor. It had been a local village of the Town of Huntington with little authority over its own affairs. They obtained the required approval of the state legislature for a local referendum, which was held on December 31, 1870. As it turned out they were premature and did not convince voters of the merits of this form of government, which would have cost taxpayers more money. The pocket book won with 118 against incorporation and only five for it. No further attempt was made for twenty-three years, until in the depression year 1893, when Sammis took the leadership again to promote another effort, this time with many more backers and with strong electoral support by Livingston's paper. The more coordinated political campaign was combined with "promises of work for all who wanted it if the project went through."[63] The proponents carried the day in the referendum on December 19, but only just barely, by 217 in favor to 212 against. Babylon's first mayor was elected in 1894. Sammis's leadership had played a large role in securing the new form of governance for his hometown.

Two short statements written by close acquaintances after his death best describe Sammis's personality and character. Henry Livingston in his newspaper obituary said, "Personally Mr. Sammis was a popular man. He was of a genial temperament and made a host of friends. He was a man who took strong likes and dislikes, and was as firm as a friend as he was uncompromising as an enemy. He made more friends than enemies, however, and even the latter could not fail to admire his enterprise, his courage and his liberality.[64] The second was written by Benjamin P. Field in 1911, some years later. Field came to Babylon about the same time that Sammis returned there from New York to start the Fire Island resort. He called himself a tinsmith, which was his principal occupation, as well as that of plumber. His place of business advertised plumbing, gas fitting, stoves, ranges and hot-air furnaces; he was younger than Sammis and was undoubtedly a supplier of goods to him. But Field was also a historian, an author and a poet, and his *Reminiscences of Babylon*, which he completed in 1911, gives a superb picture of life in nineteenth-century Babylon, depicting it as a small village, then as a resort itself, as well as a stop on the way to the Surf Hotel. Field was one of the first to build a summer cottage on Oak Island with a few others from Babylon (see Chapter Fifteen). Field said of his friend:

> The name of David Sammis seems to be indelibly pho-
> tographed into almost everything that is or has been pros-
> perous in the village. Mr. Sammis at times proudly boasted
> that his boyhood days were spent in work, hard work, for
> little pay. Mr. S. is not alone in this, for many of America's
> prominent men and business giants, in early life, had a sim-
> ilar experience; and their experience as boys taught them
> not only the value of money, but also the intrinsic value of
> time. Possessed of an unconquerable ambition and clear
> foresightedness, Mr. Sammis reached the goal of success.
> His stores, dwellings, farmlands, hotels, etc., greet the passer-
> by at almost every turn and unmistakably speak of his suc-
> cess. No one envied him his success, but all admired his
> ambition and business qualities, for while doing for him-
> self he was also doing for others by giving employment to
> many who profited by it....
> And the same human nugget of perseverance, energy
> and self-reliance, that was often seen on the street under
> a "beaver hat" and big overcoat was the man whose early
> ideas were correct. He lived to enjoy the fullest fruition of
> his early hopes, and the name of Sammis and the "Surf
> Hotel" became favorably known all over the world.[65]

Sammis, who was born in a poor family, died with an estate of about $300,000, a relatively rich man in the Babylon community. It was left to his family, his wife, Antoinette, who died in 1902, and to his daughters. It should be remembered that a large portion of his estate came from the sale of the Surf Hotel to New York State for $210,000 in 1892. During his lifetime before that sale he and his large family were not affluent; most of his resources went back into the Surf.

He was buried in the Babylon Cemetery on Deer Park Avenue after a simple ceremony at the First Presbyterian Church. During that service places of business in the village were closed as a mark of respect for one of its leaders. His gravestone in the cemetery is substantial and the names of both his wives and all seven children are engraved on all four sides. There was an effort made later to establish a memorial for him in the form of a statue to be placed near a new town house—the site for which was donated by his daughters in 1917. But that came to naught. In promoting this effort he was described as "long Babylon's leading citizen" and the "landlord king of Fire Island."[66]

Chapter Twelve
THE END FOR THE SURF HOTEL

The real monument for "the landlord king of Fire Island" had been the Surf Hotel, but it stood for only a little more than a decade after his death and was managed by a series of resort operators. As has been noted, Charles A. Merritt was the permittee in 1894. From the following year through most of the 1890s P.T. Wall was the proprietor or permittee. There was still a goodly group of guests for the big holiday events of the summer, but a decline had set in. Then, in 1900 and 1901, A. D. Chivvis became manager for the state. In 1902 a notice in the paper said that the hotel, under new management and "entirely renovated," would open for the summer on June 27. It was signed by Captain Smith Oakley. The hotel struggled on for two more summers, but no one had been able to adequately replace David Sammis, and the state was unwilling to put more money into a losing resort.

There were some proposals suggested for entirely different uses for the property. One was for a summer camp for boys from the city who would live in part of the main building. Another was for a training ground for the State National Guard. A third was more radical, which caused the expected result. In March 1904 the New York State Commission in Lunacy, in its last report to the legislature, recommended that "the Surf Hotel and cottages at Fire Island, State Property, be hereafter used as a summer resort for the lunatics of the State, particularly those restrained (or partially restrained) at Ward's Island [in New York City] or Central Islip."[67] This provoked, of course, an enormous negative reaction on the South Shore. "No more monstrous proposition could have been concocted by any set of politicians, sane or insane," said the *Signal*. Immediately a petition to the legislature protesting the use of state land for such a purpose was organized and signed by almost every resident of the village. The report of the Commission died a quiet death in Albany. However something positive would come out of these discussions.

In 1908 the New York State legislature authorized the use of the land as a state park, in a bill signed into law on May 22 by Governor Charles Evans Hughes. It was Long Island's first state park. Not for almost twenty years would there be another. Pursuant to that law the Governor appointed the first Fire Island State Park Commission, headed by Bay Shore summer resident Edward C. Blum and four other Bay Shore and Islip members. This new commission was put in charge of determining how the park would be used to benefit the public. The Surf Hotel buildings were in poor condition after a violent storm in 1907 had swept the dining hall off its foundation, damaged other buildings on the property and entirely destroyed the boardwalks. They decided to auction off what was left of the structures and tear down the rest. After a sale that produced only $2,300 in revenues, the main building was dismantled and sections were barged to the mainland. The Surf Hotel was all gone by the end of the year. For fifty-two years—since 1856—it had stood on that section of 125 acres of land.

The Fire Island State Park Commission struggled with very little money and had some bad luck in laying out a park. With the proceeds from the auction sale and $5,000 from the state legislation they built boardwalks, a small bathhouse, a comfort station, a dock, and a water supply system for the new park, which could only be reached by boat. Then, in 1918, disaster struck again, not a storm this time but a fire. Almost all the improvements except the dock were lost as a brush fire spread from Saltaire. Due to lack of funds only temporary repairs could be made. Conditions became so dangerous for the public that in 1923 the Commissioners would have closed the park except for a last minute grant of $2,000. That was the nadir, for in the following year the Long Island State Park Commission was authorized to replace the Fire Island

State Park Commission and Governor Al Smith appointed Robert Moses to head it. In 1924 the new era began for Fire Island State Park.

The first step taken by Moses, arguably his most important for Fire Island, was to press the federal government to turn over to New York State the land that had "grown" to the west of the lighthouse since 1858 when it was built, some 600 acres of new barrier beach. He was successful in acquiring this large addition to the former Surf Hotel property. It would later become the heart of Fire Island State Park and today extends two more miles to the west. Only the land west of the lighthouse is open now to the public.

PART II
OTHER
GREAT SOUTH BAY
HOSTELRIES

Chapter Thirteen

ISLANDS NORTH OF THE BARRIER BEACH

In the latter part of the 1870s other hostelries besides the Surf Hotel and Dominy House were started on the South Beach as well as on the islands to its north and on those west of the Fire Island Inlet. By then, the worst of the depression following the Panic of 1873 was over, and the success of the Surf Hotel showed that there was a demand for lodging. Some hotels grew out of restaurants and were the start of small communities. Others were stopping off places for fishing boats, and still others attracted resort guests. None ever became as large and successful as the Surf Hotel.

A word follows about the islands to the north and west of Fire Island Beach, which were once washed by the surf before being overlapped by the westward movement of sand (see Chapter One). These include East or Carabus Island, Middle Island, West Island (once two islands), Sexton or Short Beach Island and Captree Island. In the 1850s when the second lighthouse was built, Whig Inlet, which separated Sexton and Captree Islands, led directly south to the Fire Island Inlet, so that the southwest point of Sexton was at the east side of the Inlet and the southeast point of Captree was at the west side. To the west of Captree was a second group of islands, all also washed by the surf: Oak Island Beach, Muncie Island and Cedar Island. North of Oak Island Beach was Oak Island. These were separated by small inlets or waterways. All of these islands have changed in shape dramatically in the 300 years since they were first seen and mapped by early explorers. Generally, as the Fire Island Inlet moved westward, overlapping the islands, they became smaller, mostly through erosion, but also by acts of man. Captain Charles Suydam reported that in his lifetime (1880–1947) East Island had been "reduced from about ten acres to a bare acre today [1942]"[68] It has now almost all disappeared. Maps of 1900 show Middle Island being much larger than it is today and show West Island in two parts, separated by a narrow waterway running east and west. This was later filled in by a developer. Sexton Island was larger then as well.

The complex of Captree, Oak, Muncie and Cedar Islands have changed more radically than the others since they have been overlapped by Fire Island Beach. While this was occurring, the dredging of the State Boat Channel to Jones Beach in the late 1920s and then the construction of the Ocean Parkway in 1933 altered the islands to what they look like today. The small West and Cedar Island Inlets were filled in. Muncie Island disappeared forever under the sand by the building of the parkway. The bridge and causeway across the Great South Bay to Captree State Park that opened in 1954 has changed Captree Island and Oak Beach from isolated, backwater communities of several islands linked by marsh to being easily reached by automobile.

None of these islands were ever a part of the grant to William Tangier Smith (see Chapter Seven). At one time the Town of Islip, which did not receive any part of the Smith patent, claimed all the islands from East Island west to include Captree, Oak Island and part of Oak Beach. A dispute with the neighboring Town of Huntington (Babylon today) was settled in 1818 with the agreement that the dividing line would run from Sampawams Creek, the Babylon-Islip border on the mainland, south toward the lighthouse through the middle of Captree Island. Thus today Oak Island and Oak Beach are in Babylon, Captree is split, and Sexton and all islands to the east are part of Islip.

Chapter Fourteen
CHERRY GROVE, CAPTREE AND SHORT BEACH ISLANDS

On Fire Island south of Sayville in 1868, Archer and Elizabeth Perkinson started a restaurant on leased land, which became an attraction for those wanting to sail across the bay for a seafood meal. Ten years later in the Partition of Fire Island (see Chapter Seven) they purchased property near a stand of wild cherry trees and built a two-story hotel. They called it Cherry Grove. The hotel and restaurant became a success and were passed on to their son Stewart in 1895. A few private houses were barged across the bay by Sayville residents and soon a small community had started in an unplanned way.

Similarly, to the east at Water Island, opposite Blue Point, a restaurant called "Pavilion" operated by Richard Silsbee was featured in a 1878 newspaper advertisement. This was a forerunner of the White House Hotel built by Edward Ryder in 1890, a destination that became a favorite for Bayport and Blue Point summer residents such as the Roosevelts, Suydams and Posts. These two establishments could be reached more easily from the eastern part of the Great South Bay, and ferry service out of Sayville became available.

CAPTREE ISLAND
Captree Island, on a direct path from Babylon and Bay Shore through Whig Inlet to the Fire Island Inlet, was always a prime site for a hostelry. It was likely not chosen by Dominy or by Sammis because of a lack of firm ground on which to build. Captree, mostly marsh and small islands of sand connected by waterways, was more vulnerable to flooding during storms. Extensive dredging and sand fill would have been

required to create the firm space that Sammis wanted in 1855. Furthermore, as the main inlet moved west, a hurricane could have destroyed Captree completely. Nevertheless it was an excellent site for a single building, and that is why Jesse Conklin from Babylon built his restaurant, Uncle Jesse's Place, there in the early 1870s. (See Chapter Three).

On a similar Captree site across a small cove to the south of Jesse's Place the Whig Inlet House was built in 1877. This was also a single building very near the ocean entrance on the southeast corner of the island. Its proprietor, B.T. Stone, was able to attract some guests for overnight stays, just as Felix Dominy had done many years earlier. The Whig Inlet House stood on a high dune built with sand washed in from the ocean and had a fine view out to sea. Two years later it attracted the attention of an affluent New Yorker whose family had acquired wealth in the sugar refining business and whose father had been Mayor of New York three times. This New Yorker decided he would make the Whig Inlet Hotel his private seaside villa, the first instance of a summer house being built on the Atlantic beaches of the Great South Bay.

Henry Havemeyer was the fourth son of Mayor William F. Havemeyer of New York City. Born in 1836, he was by nature an adventurer and an entrepreneur. He married Jennie Moller, the daughter of another sugar refiner who had for a time been in partnership with his uncle. They would have six children. Henry, however, never went into the sugar business. After the death of his father in 1874 he became much concerned with his family's large interest in the Long Island Railroad, which was in a bad state of disorder at that time. He accepted the railroad presidency in May 1875 and improvements did take place as he promised. However the following year the Poppenhusen family took over control and Havemeyer resigned.

Babylon had come to his attention during the 1870s as an interesting area in which to build a summer home. Many of his peers had chosen the south side of Long Island by then. The same year that he acquired the Whig Inlet Hotel (1879) he was also a bidder against Franklin H. Kalbfleisch of

Babylon for the rights to lease about four miles of the South Beach west of the Oak Island Club (Oak Beach today) for a period of twenty years for development purposes. He proposed to build several resort hotels along this four-mile stretch that would be connected to the mainland by a causeway over which the Long Island Railroad would run. The Babylon Town Board awarded the leases to Kalbfleisch, announcing that he would have the "privilege" of building a bridge across the bay from Babylon to Oak Island. Nothing ever came to pass. No bridge was ever built until the Captree passenger car bridge was built in 1954. The entrepreneur was probably discouraged by the large storms in August 1879 and in November 1880.

Havemeyer called his summer home on Captree Island "The Armory." It is not known why he chose such an odd name, but he was known to be eccentric. In order to promote the Long Island Railroad he built an iron pier out into the ocean at Rockaway Beach as a tourist attraction, but lost a great deal of money on this speculation. "The Armory" was described in some detail in an article entitled "Queer Old Island Place Built By Havemeyer Sold," written in 1905, twenty-five years after Havemeyer left it. Excerpts are quoted here:

The Havemeyer Point Inn [formally The Armory] adjoining the Wa Wa Yonda Clubhouse was sold on Tuesday [July 29, 1905] to Mr. Van Allen, proprietor of the Casino, Bay Shore and other hotels. He installed service and reopened the house for the season. Havemeyer Point Inn was originally built [1879] by the late Henry Havemeyer for his private summer residence, at a cost of $150,000, on grounds leased from the Town of Islip for 99 years at a rental of $98 a year, replacing the old beach hotel. He set to work at once to improve the place. In the first place he bought a $1,500 brass clock and placed it in a beautiful $8,000 tower building on the outside of which the announcement of "BAR" still appears.

The first floor was devoted to billiards, pool and bowling, the alley for the last being considered the finest on the Atlantic coast. About the tower, which is baronial in architecture, he dug a moat and over the latter flung an arching bridge of graceful rustic construction. The interior of the old beach hotel he converted into an imitation of a ship's dining-saloon and staterooms. The most expensive woods, such as black walnut, were used in the dining room ceiling, and antique mahogany sideboards, fine glassware, etc. in furnishing it. A wine cellar was dug beneath the main building and half a dozen annexes, such as icehouse, laundry, grillroom, etc. were attached to the kitchen. Separate buildings were erected for use of a gymnasium, barn, hennery, servant's quarters, etc. Mr. Havemeyer spent $150,000 in improvements, a large portion of which was necessary to make new land in accordance with his personal ideas. For this purpose thousands of cartloads of soil were transported thence in vessels from the suburbs of New York City and a small army of men was employed on the job. Nothing was too elaborate for this "prince of good fellows" as he was commonly called. His banquets, given in the spacious dining room of the main building are still a subject of comment.

On occasions when dinners and parties were given, the main house was lavishly decorated from roof to cellar. He employed a dozen more servants about the place who were often rigged out as soldiers, armed with rifles and bayonets when guests were expected.

Four hundred feet back of the house was a beautiful lagoon, connected with the inlet by a deep creek, wherein sailboats could lie overnight or during a storm. A dock was built in this for rowboats. In the lagoon were eels, crabs, and hard and soft clams in profusion, and some oysters. The salt meadows around it were the haunts of duck, snipe, and meadow hens.[69]

The *Brooklyn Eagle* added, "Havemeyer has on the island what he calls his museum—a collection of odds and ends brought from all parts of the world which are likely to strike a person as being unique or singular. There are statues with heads knocked off, the skeletons of birds, Indian weapons, old coins, stuffed animals of which neither Havemeyer nor anyone else appears to know the names, and such a conglomeration of out of the way articles that it is naturally surprising how he has managed to get them all together."[70]

Henry Havemeyer's Armory was not only the earliest private home of a summer resident on any of the islands of the Great South Bay (he and his family lived in New York City in the winter), but it was used for a very brief time. Completed in 1879, it was occupied by him that summer and possibly part of the following one. His family never joined him there. In 1880 he purchased the 160-acre Bergen estate on the south side of Montauk Highway in West Islip, where the Good Samaritan Hospital is today, near other summer residents such as the Wagstaffs and the Clydes. Here his family could enjoy a more normal summer life. He persuaded the Argyle Hotel to rent his Armory for the summer of 1883. It was used as an annex to the main hotel in Babylon across Argyle Lake from the railroad station. During that summer President Chester A. Arthur and some members of his cabinet arrived by steamer to spend several days vacationing there. This venture was unsuccessful for the Argyle and it was unoccupied until 1885 when it was again open to the public as a resort hotel managed by proprietors Jesse Smith and George Larned. Its name was changed to Havemeyer Point House, by which it continued to be known for many years under the management of different proprietors. After Havemeyer's unexpected death in 1886 the Havemeyer Point House was sold for $12,500 to John M. Baylis, a man of "not a little experience in managing shore resorts."[71] The Babylon paper then described it as "a quiet, well-kept and thoroughly enjoyable retreat, and those who have never spent a day or a week there do not know what they have missed."[72]

It continued into the new century. In 1901 on Labor Day weekend twelve parties were listed as arrivals there, one from Philadelphia and another from Massachusetts. It was then known as the Fire Island Country Club. The last news of this hostelry was a notice of its sale to Mr. Van Allen of Bay Shore in July 1905. Apparently over the years little had been done to repair the house until 1903 when the proprietor Dr. M. M. Miller "practically rebuilt the main building, altering it from a story and a half to a two-story structure, and by putting in a complete system of plumbing, [which] not only reclaimed the place, but adapted it to hotel purposes."[73]

Most likely the end came during World War I in 1917–18 when few people went to resorts. With the building of the State Boat Channel and the Captree Island basin in the late

1920s, the land was so changed around Havemeyer Point that the structure disappeared forever.* Today the name of the point is not on any map or chart. Only very old-timers remember Havemeyer Island or Havemeyer Point, now part of Captree State Park.

One other group of buildings—a hostelry of sorts that outlasted both Castle Conklin and the Armory —was built on Captree Island in the late 1870s. It was named the Wa-Wa-Yanda Fishing Club. The origin of the name is a mystery. The early members claimed it was Indian, but it seems more likely that a member thought of it as being "far, far away" from Babylon where the ferry would depart. In any event the club was organized in New York City on May 13, 1878, as a private club by three New York businessmen: Shepherd F. Knapp, Charles Banks and William C. Conner. Knapp and Banks were members of the South Side Sportsmen's Club in Great River and had summer homes in Bay Shore. Both were excellent bird shots and wanted a club where the duck shooting, bluefishing and sailing could all be combined. Captree filled that bill perfectly.

A two-story frame clubhouse thirty by sixty feet in size was soon built on the northeast quadrant of the island facing the west end of Short Beach Island across the narrowest part of Whig Inlet. It was built on wooden piles driven deep into the marsh and connected by a boardwalk, also built on piles, to Jesse Conklin's Place, where meals were often taken by the members. The clubhouse had parlors on the ground floor and bedrooms above. Other buildings were added later for dormitories. The membership in the first year was about sixty men, principally from New York and Brooklyn, who enjoyed fishing and bird shooting as a recreation at a time when there were no limits on the catch or the shoot. The club owned two steam yachts to take members back and forth to trains at Babylon during the summer and fall seasons when it was open.

---

* It is said that the house may have been moved to the Oak Beach community nearby.

A completely bachelor establishment, it was described in 1880, the year after it opened, as "young and charming...the Wa-Wa-Yandans fish, hunt, and sail for amusement and health, and a half-dozen boats belonging to the club are kept pretty busy in the fair days of summer. The members boast of cool breezes when New York is mopping its forehead in agony."[74]

In addition to these larger buildings, Captree had numerous fishing shacks and duck hunter's blinds dotting its generally marshy landscape. These shacks went back to an earlier time when the islands were a prime source for cutting salt hay that grew naturally from the soil. "It was on the meadows at Oak Island [and Captree] and the Beaches where farmers from nearby used to harvest salt hay in August and September," said Babylon historian Benjamin P. Field in 1911.[75] The land was leased from Babylon and Islip and the cut hay was taken by barge to the mainland to be used in winter for cattle fodder and for insulation of houses. The farmers built shacks to live in during the harvesting season. Later more substantial shacks were built on both Captree and Sexton Islands where fishermen lived during the season to shorten the trips across the bay to the mainland. A community of commercial fishermen was formed on an island known as Fisherman's Island, their shacks connected by boardwalks over the marshy ground. This continued until the State Boat Channel was built, of which remnants exist today to the north of the channel entrance.

There was one other group that once had a brief visit to Captree Island for only a day and night in June 1878. However, they were so different from any other group that their story is worth recounting, as their outing was typical of a colony of artists in the nineteenth century.

The Tile Club was founded in 1877 in New York City by a very small group—only twelve—of gifted artists and writers. The name of the club was chosen to capitalize on the growing popularity of ceramics and tiles following the Centennial Exposition of 1876 held in Philadelphia. Decorative art was gaining influence in America and soon (1879) Louis

Comfort Tiffany, Samuel Coleman and Lockwood de Forest would join together to establish the firm Associated Artists. However, the original twelve Tile Club members included painters, a sculptor, several illustrators, an architect, two newspaper writers, and one person who considered himself able to practice all of these art forms. They were generally young and only Winslow Homer was considered well established at this point. Later Napoleon Sarony, Stanford White, Augustus Saint-Gaudens, William Merritt Chase and J. Alden Weir would join the Tile Club. The group met weekly at the studio of a member in New York to discuss artistic trends and other related subjects, such as what form of decorative art to pursue. Winslow Homer, more adventuresome than the others, painted tiles that he exhibited at the Century Club in New York and among friends at his studio.

In June 1878 the group planned a trip to Long Island to paint at different locations, the last of which, East Hampton, was where Homer had visited earlier. One member called it "a journey in search of the picturesque."[76] On June 10, eleven members set forth on the Long Island Railroad from Hunter's Point in Queens.

Attending were O'Donovan, Laffan, Gifford [R. Swain Gifford], Paris, Abbey, Reinhart, Smith, Quartley, Wimbridge, Shinn, and William Baird, a well-known baritone singer who had been elected honorary musician member. As this was the club's first trip, the members dressed "incongruously," and were very conspicuous with their cumbersome painting gear. Amused by the sight, O'Donovan described the group as having "a very tiley appearance."

Laffan, as a railroad employee (and conduit for free passage), was quite naturally their guide as they boarded the train en route to Babylon, where they would catch a boat to Captree Island, off Long Island's south shore. Braced against inclement weather and buoyed by high spirits, the club managed to engage the services of the sloop Amelia Corning to deliver them to Castle Conklin, an ironic name for a hodgepodge of connected clapboard structures overseen by its proprietor, Uncle Jesse Conklin. At sunrise the industrious Gifford was among the first "out hunting for a sketch," which he titled "Morning at Jesse Conklin's" [see photograph]. As the weather cleared, the others appeared, "intent and studious persons, bending assiduously over [watercolor blocks or sketchbooks]; some seated in chairs; others on the backs of them; some on sketching stools; others on boxes or in holes in the sand."[77]

In the afternoon the group left Captree Island for Sayville and then Lake Ronkonkoma for the night. The following day their journey ended in East Hampton, the main destination for their first outing together. From it came several paintings portraying scenes of the journey including Gifford's *"Morning at Jesse Conklin's"* which captures what that early hostelry looked like in 1878.* The Tile Club was the first group to give incentive to the Long Island art colony movement.

SHORT BEACH ISLAND
Across Whig Inlet from Jesse Conklin's place and the Wa-Wa-Yanda Club on the southeast corner of the island was the location of the Short Beach Club, founded in 1887. A clubhouse was constructed on the site of a hostelry that had been built by John Donnelly from Babylon in the 1870s and had burned down earlier that year. It was directly north of the Fire Island Lighthouse and within easy reach of the inlet. Its membership was quite different, however, from that of the Wa-Wa-Yanda Club nearby, and its focus was different as well.

The founding members of the Short Beach Club were Harry B. Hollins, Schuyler L. Parsons, Edward S. Knapp, John H. Vail, John Snedecor, Benjamin K. True and Harry I. Nicholas, all residents of nearby communities. All except Vail and Snedecor were also residents of New York City. With a few exceptions they or their parents had come to Babylon, West Islip, Bay Shore, Islip, Great River, Oakdale, Sayville and Bayport after the Civil War to establish summer homes for their families, making that area a socially prominent resort in the so-called Gilded Age. They estab-

---

* A chronicle of this journey to Long Island in 1878 appeared in *Scribner's Monthly* February 1879, entitled "The Tile Club at Play." The Tile Club ceased to exist in 1887.

lished social clubs on the mainland near their homes and the Short Beach Club on Short Beach or Sexton Island as it was later called. The Wa-Wa-Yanda Club membership did not have homes along the bay, by and large, and was larger and less exclusive in nature. The focus of the Short Beach Club, which never had more than seventy members, was primarily sailing and swimming or recreational fishing out the inlet nearby. It was a perfect location for all these activities. In an article about the club's opening day activities the clubhouse was described as:

...a large, comfortable and fine appearing structure, built in the Queen Anne style of architecture and surrounded on four sides by wide piazzas. The rooms on the first floor comprise parlors, dining hall, butler's pantry, kitchen and storerooms, with a wide hall, out of which the stairway to the second floor extends.

On the upper floor are numerous sleeping apartments for the club members. The rooms throughout the building are furnished in excellent taste, and the members are to be congratulated upon the comfortable and tasteful air which pervades the entire establishment.[78]

At the opening party music was played by the Seventh Regiment Band from New York, and dinner was served under the supervision of Jesse Smith of the firm Smith and Larned who had taken over Havemeyer's Armory that same year. The club elected as its first president Harry B. Hollins of Meadowfarm in East Islip, the man who made his fortune as stockbroker for William K. Vanderbilt of Idle Hour.

The Short Beach Club closed in 1912, twenty-five years later. The membership dwindled and those early opulent times began to disappear.

Chapter Fifteen
OAK ISLAND

In the earlier part of the nineteenth century, Oak Island, like all the islands along the barrier beach, was a source of salt hay "mowed by men who used scythes, taking the hay into hay cocks which were loaded into boats and sailed or poled to the mainland. Great value was placed on the salt hay in those days."[79] The towns of Babylon and Islip protected the islands for the hay farmers by seldom leasing the land for other purposes. In November 1878, however, the Babylon Town Board made an exception to that policy by authorizing twenty-one year leases for residences on Oak Island after a request from several influential Babylon men who desired to build summer cottages there. It was the best location for them being near the ocean, but not directly on the beach. In the following year two houses where built, a start to the first summer residential community on any of the Fire Island barrier beaches. It was the same year that Henry Havemeyer converted the Whig Inlet Hotel into his Armory and that the Wa-Wa-Yanda Club opened on neighboring Captree Island.

The first house was built for a social club with the lengthy name of Oak Island Beach Oyster Planters and Business Men's Association, one of the founders of which was Babylon Town Supervisor Charles Duryea. The second, also built in 1879, was for the owner and editor of the Babylon newspaper *South Side Signal*, Henry Livingston. In 1883 Benjamin P. Field built his house and in the following year Charles Searle and Alanson Weeks joined the small group of pioneers. Other houses built in the 1880s were owned by J.B. Cooper, F.S. Thorpe, J. Robbins and W.B. Lewis, all from Babylon. These houses were all in a row on the south side of Oak Island facing the ocean across Oak Beach. Each had its own dock at the end of the planks built on piles that ran out to bay. It was the only way they could be reached from the mainland, by some kind of boat (see photograph). These early owners gave their summer cottages formal names: Field's was called Arlington, Livingston's Little Rest, Weeks' Hickory Hall. The tradition continued when in 1894 John S. Foster of New York and Babylon bought Weeks' house, greatly enlarged the small shack, and called it Alabama. It was completed in 1896.

John S. Foster was the son of William R. Foster, who had come to Babylon in about 1870 when many other successful merchants were coming from New York and Brooklyn to establish summer houses in the areas from Babylon to Bellport along the Great South Bay. The senior Foster had been born on Long Island and came to New York as a young man to go into the flour trade on Canal Street. He remained in that business for forty-five years and was very successful. He had a reputation for great integrity. He was also active in Manhattan real estate, built several buildings, and was considered an expert in real estate evaluations. After his arrival in Babylon he continued to acquire property and soon became the village's largest landowner. The Fosters built their houses on Little East Neck Road south of the Montauk Highway and dredged an arm off West Creek for their yachts, which is called Foster's Creek today.

John S. Foster was the second son in the family. Expansive by nature and well-off due to the success of his father, he owned large yachts. One of these was sixty-foot schooner named *Comfort*, which he owned at the time he expanded Alabama on Oak Island. He was thought of as "a big man in those parts" of Long Island.[80]

Foster's expansion of the cottage Alabama turned what was little more than a gunner's shack into a three-story cottage and a recreation annex that included a bowling alley. Not satisfied with that, he bought a second house on Oak Island next door to Alabama, and in 1907 a third for his son, Jay Stanley Foster. In those early days there was no limit on the number of lots that one could lease. It was later restricted

When not at the Surf Hotel, Sammis, his wife, one son and six daughters lived in Babylon. Their house on East Main Street was built in 1790 as a place of worship. It became the Sammis home in 1838. *Courtesy of* Images of America.

Benjamin P. Field, Sammis's friend, Babylon tin smith, merchant, plumber, inventor, historian and writer of *Reminiscences of Babylon*. He is pictured to the right and his store below. He was also an early home owner on Oak Island. *Courtesy of* Images of America.

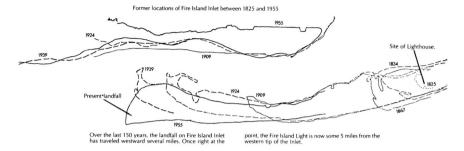

Former locations of Fire Island Inlet between 1825 and 1955

Over the last 150 years, the landfall on Fire Island Inlet has traveled westward several miles. Once right at the point, the Fire Island Light is now some 5 miles from the western tip of the Inlet.

Map of locations of the Fire Island Inlet between 1825 and 1955. *Courtesy of the Fire Island Lighthouse Preservation Society.*

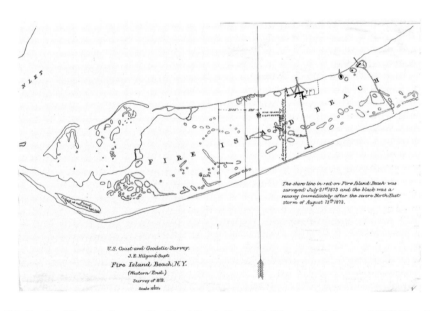

U.S. Coast and Geodetic Survey - Fire Island Beach, New York (Western End) Survey of 1873. Note that the inlet then was less than two miles west of the lighthouse and east of where the Coast Guard station is located today. This survey also shows both the Surf Hotel complex just east of the lighthouse and the Dominy House the eastern most black dot. The Fire Island Life-Saving Station is to the west and south of the lighthouse. *Courtesy of the Fire Island Lighthouse Preservation Society.*

The Tile Club of New York came to Captree Island on June 10, 1878 to sketch the local scene. They spent the night at Uncle Jesse Conklin's place. The next morning the artist R. Swain Gifford painted a watercolor and gouache *Morning at Jesse Conklin's* pictured above. *Courtesy of* The Tile Club and the Aesthetic Movement in America *by Ronald C. Pisano.*

WA-WA-YANDA FISHING CLUB

(CAP TREE ISLAND)

Babylon, N. Y. *190*

n early 20th century view of the Wa-Wa-Yanda Fishing Club on Captree Island. It was located directly orth of Jesse Conklin's place. Built in 1879 by a membership of New Yorkers who enjoyed fishing and unting, it was destroyed by the 1938 hurricane. *Courtesy of the Babylon Historical Society.*

A postcard of Oak Island mailed in 1910. The Ralph D. Howell house is at the far right and stands today *Courtesy of Ralph Howell Jr.*

The paddle-wheeler steam ferry *Oak Island* with passengers from the Babylon town dock. The ferry r: to Oak Island and Oak Beach until about 1910 when it was replaced by *Henry Ludlow*. *Courtesy of t. pamphlet "Babylon Village".*

The Channel, Oak Island, N.Y. a postcard showing the ferry *Oak Island* approaching the dock. *Courtesy of* Images of America.

...e double-decker, propeller driven ferry *Henry Ludlow* in 1913 en route to Oak Island and Oak Beach ...ich could only be reached by ferry. *Courtesy of* Images of America.

The Ocean View House, Oak Beach, N.Y.

The Ocean View House, Oak Beach, N.Y., open as early as 1879. It was located on the beach facing the Atlantic Ocean where guests could swim in the ocean surf. *Courtesy of* Images of America.

Oak Island Hotel, Oak Beach, N. Y.

Van Nostrand's Pavilion on Oak Beach facing the channel to Oak Island. It was operating by 1900 along with the Oak Beach Hotel, a more elaborate hostelry pictured below, also on Oak Beach. *Courtesy of* Images of America.

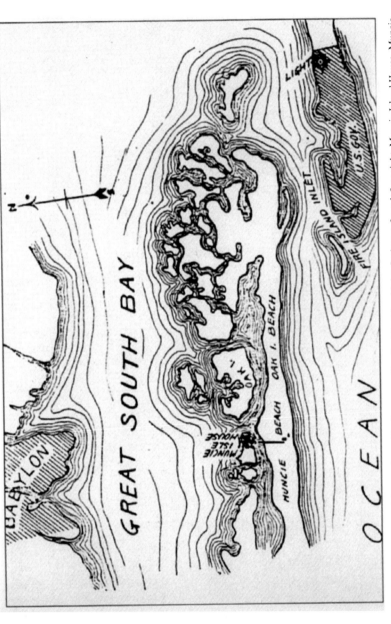

A Circa 1890 drawing of the area immediately surrounding the Fire Island Inlet. It shows, from left to right, Muncie Island House, Muncie Beach, Oak Island, Oak Island Beach, the inlet and the lighthouse. *Courtesy of* Images of America.

Towanca Jon. Muncie Island, Babylon, L.I.

A photo of the Muncie Island Hotel which Dr. Muncie operated as a sanitarium circa 1890 to 1915. Ferries ran there from the Babylon dock. *Courtesy of* Images of America.

The side-wheeler steamboat *Connetquot* purchased from William K. Vanderbilt in December, 1894 to take passengers from Sayville to Point O' Woods. She was built with a steel hull and was 78 feet long. *Courtesy of the Point O' Woods archives.*

A second ferry *Bay Shore*, 88 feet long with a wooden hull and powered by a steam driven propelle commissioned in 1895 to run to Point O' Woods from Bay Shore, stopping en route at the Surf Hotel. Th was the first ferry to leave from Bay Shore harbor. *Courtesy of the Point O' Woods archives.*

A view of people leaving the Auditorium at Point O' Woods after a lecture. It was reported in *Harper's Weekly* to seat 4000 people and to have room on the stage for a chorus of 500. Note the many parasols to protect the ladies from the hot sun. *Courtesy of the Point O' Woods archives.*

Point O' Woods, 1894-A view of the main boardwalk looking northwest, the toll house with a turnstile at the far left and the dock with many large and small sailboats which have arrived for the Chautauqua program that day. *Courtesy of the Point O' Woods archives.*

The Point O' Woods dock in 1895 with the ferry *Bay Shore* at the end. Note the ladies' dresses. *Courtesy of the Point O' Woods archives.*

Fire Island, L. I.

A postcard view circa 190C showing a large three-maste schooner at anchor off the Su Hotel. From left to right are th main hotel building, Albai cottage and the black and whi striped lighthouse. *Courtesy the Fire Island Lighthou Preservation Society.*

Two gaff-rigged sloops becalmed in the bay in front of the lighthouse. *Courtesy of the Fire Island Lighthouse Preservaton Society.*

FIRE ISLAND LIGHT

COPYRIGHT 1905, BY OVERTON, PHOTO, BABYLON, N. Y.

A 1905 postcard of the Fire Island Lighthouse with the keeper's house to the left and the generator station to the right. *Courtesy of the Fire Island Lighthouse Preservation Society.*

The West Island Casino built as a hotel in 1927 with twenty guest rooms on the southwest side of the island. Note the Fire Island lighthouse in the distance. The 1938 hurricane destroyed the Casino, the dock and most of the houses ending ferry services there. *Courtesy of* The West Fire Island Story.

An aerial view of West Island in the 1980s. Only a handful of families remained after the island was taken over by the National Park Service. *Courtesy of* Newsday *September 5, 1981.*

The Fire Island Lighthouse in 1981. It had been closed and for several years was much in need of maintenance. *Courtesy of the Fire Island Lighthouse Preservation Society.*

The Fire Island Lighthouse in 1988, open with its signal flashing again in the care of the Fire Island Lighthouse Preservation Society. *Courtesy of the Fire Island Lighthouse Preservation Society.*

to one per person. The paper speculated that John Foster owned these houses for gunning, which was popular then as now, but on which there was no limit to the number of birds killed nor on when they could be shot. A feature unique to Alabama was the location of the outside privy. Foster had the side porch arranged so that it could be reached without stepping outside into the rain. He was always considerate of his many guests. Alabama survived Foster and another owner until it was struck by lightening in June 2001 and burned to the ground.

There were other early leaseholders, some with multiple lots. Cooper had two lots on the western part of the island, as did Jeremiah Robbins and Alfred Harris. In 1900 George Mott built a house on the easternmost tip of land, giving the name of Mott's Point to that end. This house later was purchased in 1960 by Ralph D. Howell Jr. for his family and called Point Breeze. Next door to the west was the so-called Tower House (see photo) built by Jeremiah Robbins and owned after 1930 by Ralph D. Howell Sr. Father and son of the famous construction firm of E. W. Howell & Co. of Babylon lived side by side for a time. Ralph Sr.'s brother Elmer Howell also had a house west of Alabama. The community grew rapidly in the 1890s and 1900s. By 1912, fifty-three leases were recorded in the Babylon records for Oak Island lots.

In the beginning, the first owners had to rely on their own boats, mostly sail, to get back and forth from Babylon with what supplies they needed. Wells for fresh water were put down to Long Island's aquifer less than fifty feet below ground, but there was no electricity and only outhouses for sewage. Around 1886 Captain Arnold with his catboat *Sarah A* began a once-a-day ferry service from Babylon to Oak Island and return. *Sarah A* was the traditional gaff-rigged Great South Bay catboat, which could have been designed by Gil Smith, famed Patchogue builder. She was wide with a large cockpit that held several people and supplies. By 1900 there were enough houses on Oak Island and on Oak Beach for a coal-burning, steam-driven ferry to operate successfully. She would have been of very shallow draft as the channels were poor;

running aground with a load of passengers on board was not an uncommon experience. As Ralph Howell Jr. related, "My dad remembered that as the *Oak Island* steamed along, a new naphtha launch would occasionally pass, and when passengers rushed to one side to view the novelty, the paddle-wheel on that down side would dig in and turn the ferry in the opposite direction. The skipper stuttered, and he would panic as he sought to warn everyone to balance passengers on both sides, frantically moving water barrels across the deck to help, and much to the delight of a ten-year-old boy."[81] *Oak Island* was followed by *Henry Ludlow*, *Ripple*, and *Amelia* in 1911. They continued in active service until the building of the Captree Bridge across the bay in 1954.

Ralph Howell Jr., who lived there as a boy with his parents from 1929 and then with his own family through 1970—for forty-one years—described summer life as "the Oak Island Experience," and he says now in his late seventies that he still has it in his dreams. The people, the way of life, the smallness of it, the lack of the most modern communications, the difficulty of getting there before the ocean parkway was built, and in some ways the remoteness and even the loneliness were what he was remembering. There has been a community on Fire Island since 1905 called Lonelyville. That name could also have been given to Oak Island.

Chapter Sixteen
OAK BEACH

In writing the story of what today is called Oak Beach, it is particularly important to understand exactly where that is in relation to its near neighbor to the north, Oak Island (which is today still an island). This can be confusing because in earlier times and on old maps Oak Beach was called Oak Island Beach, which was separated from Oak Island by water. As the topography changed with the overlapping inlet and the building of the boat channel and the ocean parkway, the names of places changed as well. Oak Beach in the nineteenth century was washed by ocean surf on its entire south side, which began at Havemeyer's Armory and ran west to the old West Inlet (only partially open and not navigatable)* then toward Muncie Island and west to Cedar Island. The northern boundary was the natural waterway—or the "Lead," as it was known—between Oak Island and Oak Beach, back to Havemeyer's Armory. There was no inside water route to the east or west until the State Boat Channel was opened in the late 1920s. The length of Oak Beach was about three miles and its width no more than one-quarter mile. Both Oak Island and Oak Beach were reached by ferry from Babylon, which passed through a channel that still exists today, crossing the Great South Bay, stopping at Oak Island and then at two separate docks at the east and west ends of Oak Beach.

The long ocean beach was an attractive site for resort hotels after it became evident that Fire Island beach would overlap Oak Beach and not wipe it away with the westward drift of sand. That had been a threat in Sammis's early time

---

* Also known as Oak Island Inlet (see Chapter One).

(1855) and undoubtedly persuaded him to locate east of the Lighthouse. As early as 1876 there was an advertisement in the local paper for "Ocean House, Fire Island, John J. Lux, Proprietor."[82] This hostelry was on Oak Beach and would later be called Arnold's Ocean View House. Lux also owned the Washington Hotel on Deer Park Avenue near the Babylon station. The Ocean House was the earliest hotel on Oak Beach.

This stretch of ocean beach was undoubtedly in the mind of Franklin Kalbfleisch and Henry Havemeyer in 1879 when they were bidding for the right to attain the leases from the Town of Babylon for the entire beachfront from the Armory west to the South Oyster Bay line (west of Gilgo Beach today). Kalbfleisch, who won the bidding, failed to proceed with any development, which could have meant hotels almost all the way to Jones Inlet and a railroad track where the Ocean Parkway now exists.

As interest in Oak Beach grew, other hostelries appeared, sometimes called pavilions. They were generally simple affairs, for day parties at first or large enough for six to eight overnight guests. One of these pavilions was called Van Nostrand's Hotel and Pavilion in front of which was a long boardwalk extending out into the "Lead" to permit boats to dock on the bayside in the very shallow water. It was located near where the Oak Beach Inn stood until its recent demise. As the name indicated, it was owned and operated by Captain Sid Van Nostrand—a "kindly old timer from Babylon whose ancestral roots went back to the early Dutch settlers on Long Island [the western end]. Captain Sid's hospitality was widely known to hordes of vacationers, fishermen and day-boat visitors. In the pre-prohibition era, Sid's Hotel thrived with fine food and drink and was widely known as a good sea-food house."[83]

Sid Van Nostrand's brother Wes and his wife Becky ran another pavilion at Hemlock Beach (west of Cedar Beach). It was called the Hemlock Inlet House and in 1876 advertised for permanent and transient boarders. Hemlock Inlet may also have been called Cedar Island Inlet, which had been opened in a storm and closed a few years later. The pavilion had been created from an abandoned life-saving station that had been wrecked in a storm and was salvaged by the Van Nostrand brothers. Captain Charles Suydam recounted, "Hemlock Beach was popular for boating parties and picnics from both Babylon and Amityville. July 4 was one of two big days at Hemlock. After the lunch baskets were emptied, tables and chairs were pushed aside in the Pavilion and Sid and Wes would get out the fiddle and banjo. Then would come the Lanciers and the waltz.

"The other great day at Hemlock was the Second Saturday in August when the colored people [sic] had their party. They would come from near and far. Just what they were celebrating I never knew, but the Second Saturday is said to come down from the Indians who held an annual beach day."[84]

There were other hostelries on Oak Beach that followed the Ocean View House and Van Nostrand's. Strong's Hotel was owned by the Bay Shore family of that name. Wessel's Hotel at the west end of Oak Beach was a bar-stop for fishermen and fishing parties. The Oak Island Hotel was actually on Oak Beach and was of a higher class than the others. And finally the Oak Beach Inn, which survived into the twenty-first century.

Around 1900, many private houses began to spring up on Oak Beach, as they had earlier in Oak Island across the "Lead," to join the hostelries that were already there. A community developed that was separate from the all-residential Oak Island. With the community of homes came a general store and post office, Briggs Store, the Oak Island Yacht Club, and even a shipyard. There was also the Life-Saving Station that had pre-dated all these newer structures and a small nondenominational chapel. Briggs Store was also a general store. They shopped for meat and vegetables in Babylon once a week, receiving orders from their customers that were picked up at the ferry dock upon their return. For this service a very small premium was asked. Refrigeration was a problem for a small general store. Food was preserved in heavy barrels buried in the cool sands under the store. There was a great reliance on staples that kept well.

The shipyard was owned and operated by Bill Resky. Bill built houses in the off season to keep busy, but during the rest of the year there were always boats to haul out and put in his large wooden boat shed for repair. It was located at the eastern end of Oak Beach, near the Inlet. Many of the original houses were moved to keep them away from changing channels of the Inlet.

The Oak Island Beach Yacht Club became the social center of the Oak Beach community.* There were galas held on holiday weekends "which provided dancing to live orchestra music. Social life at the beach throbbed with color and enthusiasm around the old Yacht Club dances and many a beach romance budded during this era. Weekends were also marked by swimming and boat races, sail and power. Rounding out the activities were the boxing matches held every so often at the Yacht club, often pitting the talents of local amateur contests such as Bill Resky and Joe Meade."[85]

By 1911 or so, after the ferry *Henry Ludlow* and the smaller *Ripple* had succeeded the *Oak Island*, service from the mainland to Oak Island and Oak Beach was combined to serve both places for many years. Meade recalls a typical daily commute:

Depending on the size of the crowd, either the *Ludlow* or the *Ripple* would leave the Government Dock at Oak Beach at 7 A.M., with stops at Oak Beach, arriving at the Babylon Steamboat Dock at approximately 8 or 8:30. The first return trip to the beach left at 10:30 A.M. where O'Shea's and Ferraro's markets made faithful deliveries of meats and produce in time to catch the 10:30 boat. Likewise, they also made deliveries to the evening boat, which left the dock at 6:00 P.M.[86]

He also comments that the ferry would occasionally respond to the wave of a late passenger on deck.

The era from about 1890 to 1914 was one of growth for Oak Island and for Oak Beach as well, although the latter started a decade later. If an observer had stood at the western end of either of these communities and gazed to the west, he or she would have seen another island not very far away with a large hotel on its eastern end. That would have been Muncie Island and the Muncie Island Hotel.

---

* The clubhouse was barged across the bay in 1907. It had been the original clubhouse for the Babylon Yacht Club.

Chapter Seventeen
MUNCIE ISLAND

Because not a single trace of Muncie Island can be seen today, not even a barren bit of marsh, few people know that such a place ever existed. It is the Atlantis of the South Beach, and not a great deal is known about it.

Seen from above as on a map, the island was shaped like the profile of a foot walking to the east. It was only a quarter of the size of Oak Island to the east and tiny compared to Captree and Cedar Islands. It was a west extension of Oak Beach except when the small West Inlet was open after severe gales and the ocean flowed through for a time. To the north of Muncie Island was the Great South Bay and to the south the Atlantic Ocean.

In the early 1890s the Muncie brothers, who were both twins and medical doctors, decided to build a sanatorium on the east end of this island, which would later bare their name. It was to be the nineteenth century's version of a health spa for those affluent enough to pay $25 per week—the Surf Hotel charged $15 per week to its residents. When the three-story building was completed it was given the name Towanco Inn, although most local people called it Muncie's Hotel (see photograph).

In addition to the main hotel building, stucco bungalows were built along the bay side of the island. All had views of the ocean, as there were no dunes to block the view along this stretch of beach. Also on the bay side the ferry dock extended out a hundred feet or so to serve the private sailboats and the two steamboat ferries, *Nokomas* and *Senecas*, that offered twice-daily service from the Babylon ferry dock exclusively to Muncie's Hotel.

The activities on Muncie were the same as those at the Surf Hotel, featuring fresh air and ocean bathing. Its promotion, however, was somewhat different, emphasizing its suitability for convalescents in a sanatorium. It also emphasized its exclusive nature as a resort. Coming at a time after the Surf had passed its prime, the Muncie Island Hotel appealed to guests that would have gone to Sammis's resort at an earlier time. It also took full advantage of the fact that its proprietor Edward Muncie was a medical doctor.

Ed Meade, whose father lived and worked at the Oak Island Beach Life-Saving Station nearby, said, "The Muncie Island Hotel was a complete resort with a large clientele from various parts of the country.... some of them widely known and treasuring [their] privacy. One of these was a rising Hollywood star of the day, Alice Brady. This lent a touch of glamour to the community and attracted other stage luminaries."[87]

From the early 1890s to well after World War I, the Muncie Island Hotel was open from June to October and was the principal resort hotel on the South Beach.* But by the 1920s the Fire Island communities had developed and places like Ocean Beach and Fair Harbor were offering competition. The end came quickly.

Along with his plans to create Long Island's largest ocean bathing park at Jones Beach in 1929, Robert Moses also planned to build an inland boat channel from the Fire Island Inlet to Jones Beach and then an ocean parkway. These all would be done with state funds. As with almost everything he planned in his long tenure as Long Island State Park Commissioner, Moses successfully completed it with public money. The plan for the State Boat Channel showed it running along the north edge of Muncie Island with the Ocean Parkway passing down the middle of the island. Little Muncie Island was doomed. In 1927 and 1928 the dredges started the destruction. Some of the bungalows were floated by barge to Amityville and other South Shore communities, but that

---

* It was open in the summer of 1892 when the Surf Hotel was under siege by baymen (see Chapter Ten).

was not practical for the hotel and other larger structures. "Some of these houses, including the Muncie Island Hotel, were ruthlessly buried under an avalanche of mud and sand by the huge hydraulic dredge *Empire State* which was dispatched by the State Park Commission [Robert Moses] to dredge the present State Boat Channel with little regard for structures or properties."[88] The two small inlets—the West and New Inlets—were also closed forever with sand. And the fill from the dredging was pumped all over Muncie Island to prepare a solid sand base for the new ocean road that opened in 1933 from Jones Beach to Captree where it came to a dead end. Muncie Island—Long Island's Atlantis—had not sunk into the ocean. It was buried deep under the sand.

CEDAR ISLAND
The westernmost island in the group between the Fire Island and Gilgo Inlets in the nineteenth century was called Cedar Island. It was similar in size to Captree and separated from the South Beach by a small natural waterway, which in the 1920s was dredged for the State Park Channel. The ocean beach to the south of it was known as Cedar Beach, a prime Babylon resort. "A sportsman's club was situated on its dunes and was widely used by its members for picnicking, clambakes, fishing and waterfowl shooting in season. It was a landmark and could be seen for miles, either from the ocean or the bay...it was probably the last of the private shore clubs before they became public lands."[89] Cedar Beach was also reached by ferry from Babylon. To the west of Cedar Beach near Gilgo Inlet and the Life-Saving Station was Wes Van Nostrand's Pavilion, referred to earlier, that was easily reached from either Babylon or Amityville by the ferry *Columbia*.

Gilgo was a functioning inlet until after 1900, although it slowly filled in, somewhat like the Moriches Inlet today. When the Ocean Parkway was built, it was covered over with sand up to the height of the road and dunes were built to the

---

* The Jones Beach Inlet is called the New Inlet on the nautical chart of 1854.

south to protect the Gilgo Beach houses. Today there are no inlets between Fire Island and Jones Beach Inlets where once there had been several.*

Chapter Eighteen
DOMINY HOUSE 1870–1903

As had been noted (see Chapter Two), Phebe Miller Dominy sold the Dominy House to Stephen Conklin in 1869 following the death of her husband, Felix, in order to devote all her attention to her new Dominy Hotel in Bay Shore village. Conklin and his wife ran the famous beach establishment for three seasons in 1869, 1870 and 1871, all the while suffering increasing competition from David Sammis's large expansion of the Surf Hotel next door. By the end of 1871, unable to pay his bills, Conklin was forced to put the property up for sale (it was likely a tax sale), and the purchaser was his neighbor Sammis. It was probable that the latter bought Dominy House for next to nothing and that he wanted to be able to control its future, so that it could not threaten the profitability of the Surf. This event began a very long period of uncertainty for the oldest hostelry on the South Beach. It would also introduce a new hotel owner to Fire Island who would outlast the well known "king." Nine months later (October 1872), Sammis sold a half interest in Dominy House to Benjamin Sire of New York, becoming an equal partner with him. From that year until 1895 when Sammis died, the two men were sometimes partners, often rivals, and always principal owners of the only two hostelries in all of Fire Island Beach east of the Lighthouse.

Benjamin Sire was born of a Jewish family in 1831 in Darmstadt, the capital of the grand Duchy of Hesse-Damstadt in the south-central part of Germany. He married Amelia, who also came from that area, before immigrating to New York and starting their family of five sons. Their eldest son, Henry B. Sire, was born in New York in 1859. Like many industrious Germans who had immigrated at that time,

Benjamin was successful, owning and managing various theaters, hotels, and the real estate on which they stood. Some of the more famous theaters were the Bijou, the Casino and the Majestic. By the time of his death he had accumulated a sizable fortune to hand over to his five sons. It is not known how Sammis and Sire first became acquainted. It is possible that Sire was an early guest at the Surf Hotel and was thus introduced to the area that would become important to his life as well as that of his sons for almost a hundred years. The relationship of the partners must have been one of senior to junior, for Sammis was thirteen years older, a locally born man with New York hotel experience, and a very successful Surf Hotel to his credit, whereas Sire was a German Jewish immigrant just beginning a career in theater management, with a failing Dominy House on the beach (for no manager could be found). It does seem that they were an odd couple.

During the next twenty years while the Surf Hotel was enjoying great popularity as an outstanding vacation resort in the northeastern United States, visited by people from as far away as Chicago and Atlanta, the Dominy House had great difficulty remaining open and indeed was closed from time to time. Sometimes, in order to attract local people who came for bird shooting, it would remain open in September and October after the Surf Hotel had closed for the season. These erratic conditions made it almost impossible to find competent hotel managers. In 1876 the *South Side Signal* reported, "The old Dominy Hotel enjoys a fair share of hotel patronage."[90] For a newspaper that usually exaggerated its comments, this one was "damning with faint praise."

Out of desperation, in 1877 Sire leased his interest in Dominy House to Sammis, his co-owner, for a five-year period, thinking perhaps that he could find a better manager or operate it as another cottage of his main hotel. The two hostelries were close enough together to have made such an arrangement possible. For a time this appeared to help. In 1879 the *Signal* said, "Dominy House is nearly full of first class people,"[91] and in 1880, "the Dominy House, while not so large as the Surf, is a very pleasant resort and has always been popular."[92] In July 1882 the *Brooklyn Eagle* stated that Dominy House was open with twenty guests from Brooklyn. During this five year period when Sammis was in charge of Dominy House (1877–1882), Sire had not absented himself from Fire Island. In the Partition of 1878, in addition to the improvements of the Surf Hotel and Dominy House mentioned earlier (see Chapter Seven), it was stated that "Mr. Sire occupies a cottage worth $2,500."[93] Sometime between 1872 and 1878 Benjamin Sire built a house of his own very near Dominy House in present-day Kismet, becoming possibly the first summer resident on all of Fire Island to own his own home. Sammis also had his own cottage on Surf Hotel grounds, built most likely with Surf Hotel funds.

At the end of 1882, Sammis's lease of Dominy House was not renewed, and for the following three years it did not open for the summer season. One can only speculate that its business had evaporated, its conditions had deteriorated, and that its two owners could not agree on what to do about it. Sammis quite obviously did not want to invest any more money in "upgrading" Dominy House when the Surf was prospering. Sire might have been willing to do so, but only if he became the sole owner. Early in 1886 they agreed that for $2,900, Sire would buy Sammis's half interest and become the only owner of Dominy House.

With Sammis out of the picture, Sire began another renovation, more expensive than past ones because the hostelry had suffered during its three-year closing. Sire decided on a new name, "The Breakers," and hired William B. Southworth to manage it for the 1886 season. Mr. Southworth had managed the Fifth Avenue Hotel in New York City. However, due to the many renovations, 'The Breakers" opened late in the season, had but few boarders, and was unprofitable that year. It was apparent that the Surf was not losing guests to its new neighbor. It was noted in the papers however that on July 18, twenty or so of the Great South Bay's more prominent summer families spent the day at The Breakers.[94] At that time they were searching for a site for a new beach club and could have been looking at Fire Island with that in mind. They settled on Sexton Island in the following year (see Chapter Fourteen).

Following this unprofitable restart, Sire tried a new name, Hotel Madison, and a new manager for the 1887 season, William T. Kitsell, an experienced New York hotel man. These efforts were met with no greater success. He tried to find new customers by chartering boats for daily trips to Fire Island to bring out excursionists from Manhattan and Brooklyn, knowing that they were unwelcome at the Surf. He advertised in newspapers, particularly the *Brooklyn Eagle*, and sponsored notable figures on occasion to attract guests. Nothing appeared to work. But Benjamin Sire never lost hope.

In the summer of 1893 it seemed like his patience might be rewarded. The Surf Hotel had been sold by Sammis to the State of New York during the cholera scare in September 1892 and did not open for the following season (see Chapter Ten). Dominy House—as it was again called—opened under the management of E. Muncy. It advertised "Dinner Served to Yachting and Fishing Parties,"[95] emphasizing its restaurant rather than its hotel. It did not seem to make a difference. The Surf was back in business in 1894 and Dominy House continued to struggle throughout all of the 1890s.

In 1897 Sire leased the hotel to D.W. Pratt, who had plans to enlarge it, but these plans most likely did not come to pass either. It is uncertain whether it was open at all from that time until 1902, although it might have been open on special occasions.

The final chapter of the Dominy House saga began in the winter of 1901 with the announcement that Benjamin Sire of Manhattan was building a large hotel on Fire Island Beach to accommodate 500 guests; it would be located on the site of the old Dominy House. In June 1902 it was reported that it would open on June 28 and be called the New Fire Island Hotel. It would have 200 rooms (not 500 as was previously reported), stand on property 400 by 2,000 feet extending from the bay to the ocean, and be managed by Robert B. Dobie and H. Arthur Cahn. The New Fire Island Hotel did open as planned and by August 9 reported "a marked improvement in business during the past few weeks and an increased number of bookings."[96] At last the Surf Hotel, which was still in operation next door, had a real competitor. It should be remembered, however, that by 1902 there existed smaller hostelries both on Fire Island to the east and on Captree, Oak Beach and Muncie Islands to the west. Competition had become stiffer and success was by no means assured.

Benjamin Sire chose the completion of the New Fire Island Hotel as the time to deed his property to his eldest son, Henry B. Sire, then forty-three years old. Undoubtedly the father wanted to hand down to his son a successful business venture, although that first year showed no evidence of that. A promotion in the *Brooklyn Eagle* on August 22, 1902, stated that five dollars would pay all expenses from Saturday evening until Monday morning—evidence of a nearly empty hotel! Hoping to entice more guests, Sire had chosen a proprietor/manager in 1902, Gustav E. Hoerle of Midland Park, New Jersey, giving him a five-year lease on the new hotel. By late May 1903, opening day was approaching and all were optimistic.

On the night of May 27 the hotel was empty except for the caretaker, John A. Bailey, who was asleep at 4:30 A.M. when smoke and then flames were noticed by the observer in the Western Union tower nearby. The *New York Times* reported:

> ...the marine observer in the tower on the island was the first to discover the flames, and he ran to the hotel to awaken the caretaker. He had to crawl on the floor to get out. Six men were mustered [from the Surf Hotel] and formed a bucket brigade. They could do nothing with the hotel, but by hard work saved the cottage of H. B. Sire near the hotel. In two hours there was nothing by a maze of ruins where the hotel had stood.
>
> The origin of the fire is not known, but may have started in the paint shop under the hotel.[97]

The *New York Herald* filed a similar dispatch of the events, adding that the loss was $150,000 and that it was not covered by any insurance.

Reaction from the Sire brothers came a day later. First, they offered a $2,000 reward for the arrest and conviction of the party that set fire to their hotel. They were convinced that the fire was set by an arsonist. Leander B. Sire, Benjamin's son, said, "There was never a case pointing so strongly to a fire bug within my knowledge."[98] Henry B. Sire said, "There is no doubt in my mind who the incendiary was, and he is a man of wealth and prominence, and he had a motive. The evidence against him is damnable."[99] Of course they did not name the culprit, but as they described him it was not the caretaker unless he had been paid to start the blaze by another who held a grudge against the Sire family. The Sires had been in newspapers a great deal for suing or for being sued in their capacity as theater owners and managers. It was clear that they had many enemies who would want to cause them damage. If the fire was caused by an arsonist, most likely the caretaker was only the tool.

Because the Sires pressed the matter so forcibly, the District Attorney arrested John Bailey, the caretaker, on the charge of arson in the second degree—to the surprise of all. He was seventy-three years old and had been in the employ of Hoerle, the lessee of the hotel, for eleven months. As it turned out, the charge was based on the testimony of a carpenter in the employ of B. Sire. This testimony, based only on hearsay and not any direct witness of events, was very weak.

After his being held in jail for a week, Bailey's trial began with about six witnesses for the prosecution, including Clarence B. Sire, Benjamin's youngest son. Following their testimony the defense attorney asked the judge to dismiss the case, which he quickly did after criticizing the District Attorney for bringing before him a case with such flimsy evidence. Afterwards, Bailey said, "It was my duty to be in that hotel. It seemed because I was in the hotel when it started to burn, the owners jumped to the conclusion that I fired it.

There was no evidence that I was in anyway responsible for the destruction of the hotel."[100] The Sire family was never able to connect the real culprit to the destruction of the New Fire Island Hotel. In spite of insisting that they would rebuild, they never did. The Old Dominy House built in 1844 was no more. It had been a landmark on Fire Island for almost sixty years. The end of the Surf Hotel would come five years later.

Benjamin Sire died on 1907 at the age of seventy-six. His wife Amelia had predeceased him. Four of their five sons lived on, enjoying the summer house that had survived the fire, and also building four or five other homes on this large piece of property. Clarence, the youngest son, took a particular interest in what came to be called Kismet. He always considered himself "from Fire Island" and for a time conducted a seaweed baling operation from the site of Dominy House, using the hotel's powerhouse that had escaped the fire. Clarence's wife, Lillian Sire, was a founder of the Women's National Democratic Club and was active in New York State Democratic politics under Governors Al Smith and Herbert Lehman.

In 1918 the brush fire that started in Saltaire burned westward all the way to the Inlet. It destroyed most of the Sire buildings in Kismet and almost all the structures in the infant Fire Island State Park, which had by then replaced the Surf Hotel (See Chapter Twelve). Clarence Sire's descendants sold much of their property to developers in 1956, which became known as Lighthouse Shores, a part of Kismet. The last Sire land went to the Fire Island National Seashore in 1966.

In Kismet today, slightly west of the boat basin and ferry dock facing the Great South Bay, a small monument has been erected on the site of the Dominy House. From it one looks north to the main channel to Bay Shore and west to the channel past the Fire Island Lighthouse toward the Inlet. The monument is made of red bricks from the powerhouse with the old mortar still attached. It is in the form of a semi-cir-

cle about eight to ten inches high. By it is a plaque inscribed
as follows:
Site of Fire Island's First Hotel
The Dominy House built in 1844 by lighthouse keeper
Felix Dominy, enlarged to 200 rooms by Benjamin Sire in
1902, burned in 1903,
bricks are the remains of the chimney of the powerhouse.
Monument executed 1989 by friends of Kismet historian
James Albert Bliss
1902 – 1989

Chapter Nineteen
POINT O'WOODS
THE CHAUTAUQUA
EXPERIMENT 1894–1897

In 1894 there were several hostelries on Fire Island and on the other islands west of the Inlet, but few groups of homes. As has been noted, there had been several summer houses built on Oak Island, mainly by residents of Babylon, and also ooveral summer bungalows had sprung up on Muncie Island near the hotel there. However, neither of these could be called communities in the fullest sense of that word, as they had not been the result of a plan that included the amenities that would attract many people for a whole summer season. At that time, except for those few who had their own boats, all came across the bay by ferry from the Babylon dock, the principal terminal on the mainland.*

This would change when "a group of respected citizens" from Babylon, Bay Shore, Sayville, Islip and Patchogue met in early March 1894 to discuss a proposed Chautauqua assembly.[101] One of the places they considered was the property of the Surf Hotel, then owned by New York State. It was a time when the state was under pressure to sell it; many local citizens did not want it used again as a quarantine station (See Chapter Twelve). They also looked at property near present-day Saltaire, which also would have been easily reached by ferry from Babylon. They were looking for space extending from the bay to the ocean and wide enough to plan for upwards

---

* The hotels in Cherry Grove and Water Island may have had boats to serve their guests that crossed the bay from Sayville.

of 1,000 building lots. There was nothing timid about the magnitude of their conception.

They settled on roughly 150 acres of bay to beach property located five miles east of the Surf Hotel. It was part of Lot 21 (the largest lot in the Partition of 1878—see Chapter Seven) and was owned by the Terry family of Sayville. Isaac G. Terry was a part of the group planning the Chautauqua assembly. In addition to its large size, the frontage was 4,000 feet. They were also attracted by the eight feet of deep water where the deck would be built. Agreement with Terry was quickly reached and by March 17 it was announced that shares would be sold to the public for ten dollars apiece. Five shares bought a ninety-nine year lease on one building lot, on which the keeper had to build within three years. Under the terms of this lease, Chautauqua's rule requiring that "no intoxicating drinks shall be used as a beverage on said devised premises, under any circumstances whatsoever,"[+] was to be followed. It was to be a completely dry community!

The formal name given to this new community was the Long Island Chautauqua Assembly. It was the only such assembly on Long Island, but it was not a new concept. A word about its history:

In 1873, twenty years earlier, two men, John H. Vincent and Lewis Miller, proposed to the Methodist-Episcopal camp meeting they were attending, that secular as well as religious instruction be included in the summer Sunday school institute for the following year and that the institute develop an eight-week summer program offering courses in the arts, sciences and humanities. The institute began this program in 1874 at a site along the west shore of Chautauqua Lake in upstate New York, taking the name of that lake—after the Indian tribe—as the name of the institute. It was a great success. Possibly two-hundred others were organized throughout the Northeast, known as Chautauqua Assemblies, but few were as successful as the original, which survives today on permanent grounds by Chautauqua Lake. The religious

---

+ Chautauqua lease is in the Point O'Woods archives.

aspect of the program was largely replaced by the secular. Anyone could attend, although most were Protestant Christians. There was something of the spirit of a revival meeting among assemblies and something of a country fair, all coming together to satisfy a thirst for education. Twenty years later this movement reached Long Island.

The group of local businessmen was headed by N.W. Foster, president of the bank at Riverhead, and the Reverend A.E. Colton of Patchogue. Also in the group were the Reverend John D. Long of Babylon, O.A. Ackerly of Yonkers, G.W. Winterburn of New York, and a number of others from South Shore villages including Isaac G. Terry of Sayville, the owner of the Point O'Woods site. Colonel J.Y. Cuyler, an experienced landscape architect of Brooklyn parks, was charged with designing the layout on the 150 acres. Time was of the essence that spring. From early March when shares in the endeavor were first sold, to July 4 when opening day was planned, was only four months. There would be no help from the home base in Chautauqua, New York. Local members had to plan everything from building to program to transportation. It seemed an impossible task to produce all this on a vacant Fire Island strip of sand, five miles from mainland Long Island.

Colonel Cuyler had to build a dock on the bayside, a boardwalk to the ocean, and an auditorium where lectures could be held. There was a question about its size. Fire Island historian Madeleine Johnson stated, "In the plans was an auditorium that could hold 6,000. It was to have a roof (and even a roof garden) but no sides."[102] Whereas *Harper's Weekly* on July 21, 1894, after opening day said, "The Auditorium, where lectures are given, is finished, and has a seating capacity of 4,000 and room on the stage for a chorus of 500." Both figures seem greatly exaggerated, but the auditorium was completed in time to start the program on July fourth. *Harper's Weekly* photographs showed a long, rectangular, wooden structure with a gently sloping roof. The school building was connected on the right and both appear to be of a single story. *Harper's* continued, "There is also a school building with thirty classrooms, the Association House, and a large number of shops and bath-houses." Much more of Cuyler's plan was never built, such as a park, athletic fields, and a university on the eastern part of the property. The Chautauquans of Point O'Woods needed houses, of course, although many attendees came for the day on their sailboats and entered through a turnstile on the dock after paying twenty-five cents each. Colonel Cuyler had laid out 1,000 building lots on his plan, of which over 250 had been sold by July 21 according to *Harper's Weekly. The South Side Signal* said that the Decker Portable House Company had received a concession for building several groups of houses, which were easily put up and taken down, no expert help necessary. And they were cool in the summer. It also said that forty-seven building lots had been assigned by May 5.[103] Thus it was clear that for the first season at least, the houses were portable and that at most there were thirty put up. Most of the participants in the formal program did not spend the night that first summer.

The program of adult education offered included lectures, concerts and classroom instruction. The lectures and concerts were held in the afternoons, usually at 1:30, 3:00 and 4:00. Class instruction was given in the morning. For the week of July 30 there were offerings of Hebrew, Semitic languages, Greek, Latin, modern languages, music, art, cooking and navigation. These were given by professors from Princeton, Chicago, Hartford and the Stevens Institute. Professors, doctors, ministers, congressmen, senators and a US Navy captain were engaged to give lectures for the season, which closed on September 5. In the evening there was either a concert or a prayer meeting at 8:00, and on Sunday at 11:00 A.M. a nondenominational church service with a sermon and at 5:00 P.M. vespers were held. Indeed the Point O'Woods Chautauqua had all the makings of a university summer school and was eagerly awaited by many.

All during the spring the local South Shore newspapers promoted the Chautauqua with almost weekly news dispatches of its various stages of development pointing to opening day on July 4. A feverish excitement grew, as there had never been such an occasion before on the Great South Bay. Johnson described it as follows:

> The great day dawned fair with a favorable wind for sailing across the bay, and at least 150 boats made the trip. The boats and their passengers were bedecked with ribbons, which flew smartly in the breeze. By noon, some three thousand people had arrived to find tents and booths lining the walk and offering refreshments and souvenirs. Unfortunately, the speakers were delayed, forcing cancellation of the morning ceremonies; so everyone went to the beach. The exercises began at 1:30 with an evocation by President Nat Foster. Congressman Burros, of Michigan, C.C. Coffin, and Mary L. Dickerson gave orations. The violinist Lewis Blumendick was listed in the program, which was to conclude with a grand concert and "installation of the first class of the American Patriotic League." The speeches and music went on and on. In the afternoon a squall threatened, and the audience became restive. Some orations and musical numbers were eliminated, and everyone headed for the boats; but the squall held off, allowing a safe sail home. All in all, despite some hitches, the day was proclaimed a huge success.[104]

Throughout the summer the New York City papers also mentioned the program held at Point O'Woods. On July 30 the *New York Times* ended its article on the "Attractions at Point O'Woods" by saying, "This resort is rapidly becoming very popular with residents of Long Island to whom it is within easy access. Boats run regularly from Babylon and Bay Shore across the Great South Bay to the beach where a delighted breeze is always blowing."[105] What it failed to say was that although many private boats—mostly sail—ran regularly across the bay, there were no ferries to Point O'Woods during the summer of 1894, an incredible oversight by the planners of the Chautauqua Assembly. A second oversight was that there was no hotel or public boarding facility, although in June the directors finally decided that one should be built. By the following year the *Suffolk County News* reported that a new hotel, the Gerard House, was built.* The lack of a pub-

---

* The 100-room Gerard House burned down in September 1909.

lic hostelry and the lack of public transportation resulted in a poor financial showing for 1894 in spite of the initial promotional and enthusiasm of so many. For 1895 the directors tried to remedy both problems.

In addition to a new hotel, the Suffolk County Women's Christian Temperance Union (WCTU) was invited to join and to build lodgings. The Ocean House opened that year with a restaurant and twenty dormitories.

As for transportation, the Chautauquans encouraged the Sayville Steamboat Company to purchase William K. Vanderbilt's steam side-wheeler *Connetquot*, which had been laid up at his dock at Idle Hour for the past two years. Mr. Vanderbilt had seldom been at his home there during that time prior to his getting a divorce from his wife Alva. The plan was that the *Connetquot* would run from Sayville to Point O'Woods for the exclusive use of the Chautauquans. She had been built in 1890 with a steel hull, was seventy-eight feet long and could carry 150 passengers. After a trial run in November 1894 (during which the rusted steering cable broke and had to be replaced), which proved that the trip would take only thirty-seven minutes dock to dock, the Sayville Company bought her for $4,000. She began service for the 1895 season.

Although Sayville is the closest mainland harbor to Point O'Woods—five miles—it is farther east and a longer trip on the train from New York than is Bay Shore. As time would tell, the overall trip from New York is quicker through Bay Shore from where the ferry now runs to Point O'Woods— seven to eight miles away. In 1895 it was fortunate that a second ferry, named *Bay Shore,* was commissioned to run to Point O'Woods, stopping at the Surf Hotel en route. *Bay Shore* was eighty-eight feet in length—a large boat—with a wooden hull and powered with a steam-driven propeller. She was reported to be the first public ferry to leave from Bay Shore harbor. All previous ferries to the beach had departed from the Babylon steamboat dock owned by David Sammis.

There are reports that a second Vanderbilt boat, the seventy-one foot side-wheeler *Mosquito,* ran from Sayville to

Point O'Woods but that was most likely after 1897 when *Connetquot* broke down in mid-summer. Also a ferry named *Grace Shaffer* may have run from Patchogue, the eastern-most port on the Great South Bay, which would have been a long trip if a visitor was coming from the city. Lastly, *Nancy Lee* may have made trips to Point O'Woods. In spite of good ferry service and the addition of a hotel, 1895 was less successful financially than 1894. Attendance was declining. It seemed as though the novelty of the Chautauqua experience was wearing off. The newspapers were loosing interest. Special efforts were made in 1896 and in 1897 to increase attendance, but nothing seemed to work. Some felt that the main problem was the prohibition against alcohol. As it turned out, July 4, 1894—opening day—was the best day the Chautauquans would have. It was downhill from there.

On January 22, 1898, the *South Side Signal* announced that the Chautauqua Assembly, to pay its debts, had voted to dispose of its property. Its stockholders—those who owned leases on lots—voted to reorganize as a business association called the Point O'Woods Association and to sell the unsold lots. The turnstile at the dock would be removed to encourage picnickers and day-trippers. A committee lead by Charles Hand, William Griffin and George Gerard found enough new stockholders to pay off the debt to the Chautauqua Assembly, persuaded Isaac Terry to take stock for the debt he held, and opened in 1898 with a clean slate. The Association owned the lease on all the land, as it does today. Homebuilders owned their houses, but not the land under them; building must be approved by the directors of the association. In the winter of 1898–99 a ferry was commissioned to be built, and ever since then the association has had its own ferry, which runs to their private dock in Bay Shore. In 1898 the Point O'Woods Association became Fire Island's first community, a successful stepchild of the Chautauqua Assembly's failed experiment.

EPILOGUE
THE 20TH CENTURY

With the beginning of a new century, development along the Great South Beach began to change from hotels to communities. The change was not abrupt, but slowly evolved. Hotels did not disappear right away—there are some in Ocean Beach today—but it was clear with the destruction of Dominy House in 1903 and the final closing of the Surf Hotel in 1908 that their day was over. This was also true of the large hotels on the mainland in Babylon, Bay Shore, Islip and Sayville. As has been noted, some fledgling communities had come into being before 1900, those at Oak Island and Point O'Woods. Another was planned for West Island in 1901 but did not materialize until much later in the 1920s. On Fire Island, Point O'Woods was followed by Cherry Grove, Lonelyville, Ocean Beach and Saltaire. To the west of the Inlet, Oak Beach also came into existence at this time. By World War I it was clear that communities of summer houses (some people would live there all year round) would describe the future of the barrier beach.

The history of the Great South Beach in the twentieth century can be divided into two parts. The first, the growth of communities, lasted until 1964, and the second, one of stability, conservation, and preservation, continues today. To conclude the story of the earlier time I will highlight some of the important events and changes of the past century.

To begin with its geography, Fire Island Beach and its Inlet have continued to move west at a rapid pace. Now more than six miles west of the Lighthouse, the Beach and Inlet overlap Oak Beach at a point opposite Cedar Beach. The Inlet is dredged by the federal government almost yearly to keep it navigable for both commercial and pleasure boats. If this was not done, it would surely join its neighbor Gilgo Inlet as a "former" inlet. Northeast storms continue to eat away at the beach, pushing sand westward. This has the effect of narrowing parts of the barrier beach and widening other sections. Much of the sand returns, however, in the summer southerlies. A northeaster in March 1931 opened a new inlet into Moriches Bay to the east, but did not reopen Gilgo Inlet to the west, probably because the dredging of the State Boat Channel had caused dunes to be built at this narrow point of the beach. It also destroyed the abandoned Western Union Telegraph tower.

The great storm of the century was, of course, the hurricane of September 21, 1938. It was the most severe hurricane to hit Long Island since the storm of 1815. A storm surge estimated to be thirty feet high caused the ocean to break through into the bay at Cherry Grove and at Saltaire. An eight-foot-wide channel was temporarily created through the latter community, but was closed quickly by great human effort after the storm had passed. More than fifty people lost their lives on Long Island, mostly at West Hampton Beach where there were no dunes to protect houses. Although the geography of Fire Island was not permanently altered that September, much that had been built was wiped away like crumbs on a table. A total of 265 houses on Fire Island were lost and 32 were damaged, some beyond repair. Kismet, Saltaire, Fair Harbor in the west and Cherry Grove in the east were hardest hit. Only one house survived in Kismet, and eight in Fair Harbor.

As well as houses, the 1938 hurricane destroyed the Postal Telegraph tower, taken out of service in 1920 due to the advent of radio, and Camp Cheerful, which had been built on the former property of the Surf Hotel. In cooperation with the State Park Commission, the New York City Rotary Club built the camp in 1926 for crippled boys. It had consisted of nine cabins, an infirmary, a mess hall, a storehouse, helpers' quarters and a bathroom. All were wiped out. A similar fate befell all park buildings, boardwalks, docks and the water supply, which Robert Moses had erected since 1924 when he became Parks

Commissioner. Nothing remained on park land but wreckage and the stalwart Fire Island Lighthouse, relatively unscathed, flashing away every seven and a half seconds. In 1939 Moses started rebuilding the park all over again, but in a new location two and a half miles west of the Lighthouse where the dunes were higher and offered more protection. These facilities were opened to the public in June 1940.

In telling the story of Fire Island's growth in the twentieth century, more must be said about Robert Moses, an important and controversial figure who, in the thirty-eight years he was Long Island State Park Commissioner (1924 to 1962), made the barrier beach south of the Great South Bay what it looks like today.

With a passion for bringing people to the beach by automobile, he planned from the beginning to connect Fire Island to the mainland by bridges and parkways. His 1927 plan showed the Ocean Parkway running east from Jones Beach, crossing Fire Island Inlet over a bridge and then down the entire length of Fire Island Beach passing Smith Point to Hampton Bays where cars could return to the mainland. Bridges and causeways would be built for cars to reach Ocean Parkway across the bay from Conklin's Point between Babylon and Bay Shore and from Smith Point as well. During his tenure, much of this plan was brought into being. All the bridges were built and the Ocean Parkway crossed the Inlet to newly named Robert Moses State Park, and then ran east to the Lighthouse where it ended! The next segment of road to Smith Point was blocked by New York State Governor Nelson Rockefeller and the people of the communities on Fire Island.*

Other accomplishments of Moses were his persuading the Congress of the United States in 1924 to pass a law turning over to New York State all federal land west of the Lighthouse, which would include all land newly built by the westward drift of sand. Thus Robert Moses State Park became larger every year since 1924 and continues to do so! To the great benefit of

---

* For a more complete account of Robert Moses on Fire Island, read Johnson's *Fire Island 1650s–1980s.*

boaters he built the State Boat Channel in 1928–29 from Jones Beach to the Fire Island Inlet, an inland waterway for small boats that connects the Great South Bay with points west without venturing into the ocean. Fill from dredging was used to build the Ocean Parkway, which opened in 1933.

Most of Moses' plans were stopped temporarily by the Hurricane of 1938 and then by World War II with its gas rationing. But by the 1950s he was on the move again. The Captree Bridge and Causeway was opened in 1954, bringing the Ocean Parkway to the mainland and connecting it with his Southern State Parkway. The bridge to Smith Point was completed by then as well.

During the first half of the century the communities grew in number and also in size. They were situated both west of the Inlet from West Gilgo Beach to Oak Beach and east of it from Kismet to Davis Park, a distance of twenty-five miles.* There were communities on the bay islands as well, on Oak Island, Captree, Sexton and West Islands. Most of these prospered and exist today. One did not.

West Fire Island, commonly called West Island, was first in the news in 1901 when Frank Buchacek, proprietor of Islip's Orowoc Hotel, was said to purchase sixty acres of West Island (the western half) from Sarah Nicoll to build an up-to-date summer hotel as a day resort. A large pier was to be built for boat landings as well as a two-story building with a dining hall, cafe, and kitchen on the ground floor and a limited number of sleeping apartments as the second floor.[106] There is no evidence that this project ever took place at this early time.

However in 1922 a group of local business men and a doctor with Fire Island roots saw the possibility of building a community at a time when housing booms had come to Long Island and new developments were springing up along the South Shore. West Island was located less than a mile north of Saltaire, which was rapidly growing by then. The distance between them could be easily traveled by boat, which would have given comfort to the developers. Since the earliest days

---

* Only communities in Suffolk County south of the Great South Bay are included.

of map making the island had been divided in two sections by a small cut or stream where duck hunters built their blinds. It was very low, with the highest point being three feet, so that houses and boardwalks had to be built on piles and were subject to flooding during storm tides. Longtime West Island resident Henry R. Bang described its development:

> In 1922, a development company with Edward Thompson, Dr. George King, Selah Clock and Edward Lyons as the principal owners was formed with the objective of building an exclusive summer resort. A great deal of money was spent building bulkheads, docks, an artesian well and a water system of three-inch pipe, which criss-crossed the island to supply several hundred houses. Miles of boardwalks were built on locust posts and topped with chestnut boards (that was before the chestnut blight) criss-crossed the island, which is only half a mile long and quarter of a mile wide. Streets with hand-carved signs bearing names such as Widgeon Way, Albatross Way, Pelican Walk and Petrel Walk marked every intersection. A twenty-room hotel called the Casino and about ten cottages were built and rented to prospective purchasers of summer houses.[107]

West Island was served by the ferries *XL* and *Kismet* from Bay Shore until the 1938 hurricane destroyed the pier. To create this community, the small cut or stream was filled in by dredging sand from the bay, creating a single island on which were laid out six streets lengthwise and five streets across its width. All of these streets were named, sometimes with the name of the homeowner.

At its height in the 1920s, perhaps fifty families owned houses on West Island. It never had electricity except for a battery that ran the water pump. Cooking was done with propane gas. Henry Bang continued:

> West Island was the place to go to be wined and dined by the developers, who were beginning to be concerned about the lack of interest of people in buying homes on the Island. The Casino was full every weekend. There were instructors to give dancing, swimming and sailing lessons. Over the fireplace in the Casino was an oak mantelpiece with the hand-carved words, "In the safe anchorage find welcome and cheer."[108]

Although the 1920s was the decade of prohibition, surely alcohol flowed freely in the West Island Casino.

The Depression ended the hope of the developers to attract more homeowners and many of the fifty families began to leave. In addition to the hard times, the lack of electricity and telephone was having its effect. Then came the hurricane, which destroyed the Casino, the dock and many houses. Some that were salvageable were moved to the mainland. Ferries stopped service, as there was no longer a pier. It was evident by 1942 when the war started that West Island was no longer a community that would grow again. In 1964 most owners (but not all) sold to the new National Seashore. Only ten or so private lots remained, but these few families were allowed to stay under the new law. They were required to keep their houses the way they were built. No new houses were permitted. Some houses have collapsed into the bay and only a few remain today.

The last community to be built on Fire Island was Dunewood in 1958. Located between Fair Harbor and Lonelyville, it was a planned community of 100 lots designed by Long Island developers Maurice Barbash and Irwin Chess. In total these occupy only twenty acres from ocean to bay. Dunewood is a family community and has been a great success. Soon thereafter the tide began to turn from development to conservation in the minds of many Fire Islanders.

The first step toward preservation took place in the early 1950s when a small group led by Richard Pough and Robert Cushman Murphy of the American Museum of Natural History in New York City began their efforts to "save" an area on Fire Island just east of Point O'Woods known as Sunken Forest. They formed Wildlife Preserves, Inc., a nonprofit institution to acquire and hold this thirty-six acre nature preserve, which would be open to the public. After substantial fundraising from private sources, the group was able to acquire Sunken Forest in 1959, saving it for posterity in its primeval state and not incidentally making it more difficult for Moses to put his ocean parkway through it.

Madeleine Johnson, who grew up in Point O'Woods next door and knew Sunken Forest for a longer time than most, described it as follows:

> Hidden behind the interdune, down in a valley on the bay side of the island about a mile east of Point O'Woods, is a primeval forest. Here, American holly trees with trunks twisted and gnarled reach heights of about thirty-five feet; here are sassafras, tupelo, post oak, red cedar and shadbark, dense thickets of cat brier and poison ivy. Three-inch-thick poison ivy vines flaunt their leaves at the tops of dead cedars that their leaves have killed by the shade they cast. The thick canopy darkens the area. This canopy is at a uniform level because the salt spray from the ocean clips off all but a few random twigs at the same height when the growth reaches the interdune. At its lowest point, the floor is almost at sea level. It is damp and covered with dark mold about six inches thick. Mostly marsh, in a few slightly open places, ferns, wild sarsaparilla, and Canadian mayflowers find footing. Raccoon, fox, and deer make their homes in this secluded area. Birds flit quietly among the branches. The sounds of wind and ocean are muted. A visit to the Sunken Forest is a dip into the palm of nature itself. Here, the vital business of survival proceeds silently and mysteriously.[109]

Sunken Forest was given by Wildlife Preserves to the Fire Island National Seashore after it had been created in 1964, thus guaranteeing its preservation even more solidly.

The next step toward preservation came about largely due to Robert Moses' attempts to continue building the Ocean Parkway from Fire Island State Park east to Smith Point where it would again connect with the mainland. His efforts had been persistent since 1924 when he became Long Island Parks Commissioner. By 1960, perhaps because he was more aware of his advancing age (he was seventy-two years old), his efforts intensified, and the parkway extension seemed inevitable. He had always been able to overcome the resistance of local citizens and New York State governors had almost always gone along with his wishes. Could the bulldozer be halted this time? In 1962 a public hearing was held, as required by law, before final plans could be sent to the New York legislature for approval. In spite of overwhelming opposition from 1,500 Fire Islanders at the hearing, the Long Island State Park Commission and the Suffolk County Board of Supervisors approved the building of Ocean Parkway and sent it on to Albany in August. The last remaining hope to stop it rested with Governor Nelson A. Rockefeller, who had never committed himself to Moses' plan.

At this point the Governor, undoubtedly encouraged by his conservationist brother Laurance, who was at that time vice chairman of the New York State Council of Parks, asked Robert Moses to resign his office as chair of that body because he had accepted the chair of the upcoming New York World's Fair, a full time job. Moses, then seventy-three, bitterly submitted his resignation from all his four state posts, including that of head of the Long Island State Park Commission, which he had held since 1924. Rockefeller quickly accepted the resignations, and for the first time in thirty-eight years Robert Moses had no authority over Long Island in any way! The state legislature then delayed any action on the Ocean Parkway to see what was transpiring in the U.S. Congress in Washington.

The concept of a Fire Island National Seashore had begun in the 1950s, but progressed slowly because it was publicly opposed by Robert Moses and earlier New York State governors. It was not until 1962 that a bill reached the floor in the House of Representatives, but died in the rush to adjourn that year before elections. Then in June 1963, Suffolk County representative Otis Pike introduced a bill to create a national seashore from Robert Moses State Park to Smith Point County Park. It included West Island and East Island, but not Sexton Island, which remained a part of the Town of Islip.* With the support of almost all groups on Long Island, the bill was passed by Congress and signed by President Johnson in September 1964. The Fire Island National

---

* In 1985 the former Surf Hotel property of 120 acres was transferred by New York State to the National Seashore in exchange for park land near Montauk Point. It had been unused since the 1938 hurricane.

Seashore Act provided that the communities could continue to develop under the guidelines already set by them within their boundaries, but that undeveloped land must remain that way. Those without clear title had to move within a few years time, and their houses were destroyed. This did cause some resentment but it was not widespread. The Fire Island Association how represents owners and works closely with the National Park Service, which is in charge of preserving and protecting the park.

Thus the year 1964 should be seen as a landmark in the twentieth-century history of Fire Island, when growth and development changed to conservation and preservation. The National Seashore became open to the public by ferry to Sailors' Haven and Watch Hill, as well as by walking along the twenty-mile barrier beach that always has been a public footpath within a hundred feet of high tide. Only a very few year-round residents and builders are allowed vehicle permits to pass along the dirt and sand path to Ocean Parkway west of the Lighthouse. Camping is permitted under the close supervision of the park rangers in certain designated sites along the dunes to the east, and Sunken Forest continues to attract many visitors who come by boat or ferry from Sayville.

Since 1964, preservation has been the central theme on Fire Island, and one of the most significant beneficiaries has been its oldest structure, the Fire Island Lighthouse. First built in 1826 and again in 1858, the Lighthouse has been the commanding feature of the entire Great South Bay area. With its light flashing every seven and a half seconds, it can be seen at night for twenty miles in every direction. Since 1939 the United States Coast Guard had been responsible for its operation and upkeep. But by the 1970s, with the advent of modern navigational devices, the need for lighthouses no longer existed and the funds of the Coast Guard had to be directed to other more vital uses. The Fire Island Lighthouse gradually fell into disrepair and in 1974 the light was extinguished and the site abandoned. In 1981 it was declared beyond repair and was slated for demolition. There seemed to be little chance for its preservation.

However, there were many Great South Bay residents who missed the flashing light and were willing to work and give money to save it for posterity, in much the same way as Sunken Forest was saved in the 1950s. The Fire Island Lighthouse Preservation Society (FILPS) was formed in 1982 to raise funds to restore the dormant lighthouse. The property was turned over by the Coast Guard to the National Park Service, which undertook its management with the support of FILPS. From then on all parties worked together with the common goal of restoring, renovating and improving this historic structure and its auxiliary buildings. Two miles of boardwalks were built, the keeper's house was remodeled into a visitor's center and small museum, and a new beacon was placed on top of the restored tower.

On the evening of May 25, 1986, at 9:00 P.M. as darkness fell on the bay, over 100 small boats patiently waited around its north side until the new beacon was lit amidst the sounding of boat horns. It was a glorious moment that those who were there will never forget. The Lighthouse, which had been dark for twelve years, flashed again every seven and a half seconds. The visitor's center was dedicated and opened to the public that day as well. The tower was opened for tours in 1989. Restoration continues. Preservation is an expensive and constant task. The Lighthouse today is in good hands and the "Old Lady" looks pretty well at 147 years of age!

Although Sunken Forest and the Lighthouse have been saved, preservation of the beach itself has been and is a continuing vital concern to the entire community, not only those residents on Fire Island but to all who reside along the Great South Bay. The barrier beach is constantly under threat of storms. Since 1964 the Fire Island National Seashore has experienced only one major hurricane, Gloria in 1985, but there have been several damaging northeasters that have carved away beach with their wind and high tides. The only real protection from these destructive forces of nature are the sand dunes built up along the entire length of the beach. Without high dunes, well maintained with beach grass to hold the sand in place, the ocean could break through with any large storm system. We have learned from experience that where the dunes are high, damage is minimized. This means, of course, that dunes must never be built upon or lowered for better views of the ocean. And the beach must be deepened upon occasion by dredging and pumping new sand from the ocean, an expensive project. Nature provides some addition of sand with the summer southerlies, but weak spots must be reinforced by mechanical means. Other than shifting sand from the ocean to the beach, no other man-made reinforcements have ever been successful.

Although most Fire Islanders are aware of these needs for preservation, and the Fire Island Association battles constantly to protect the dunes and the beach, many on the north side of the bay fail to realize the destruction that would occur to whole communities of villages if there should be several breakthroughs of the beach today. Should there be a 1938-size hurricane again, no home south of the Montauk Highway from Freeport to Bellport would escape some damage, and no marina would survive intact. This nightmare can only be avoided by keeping the dunes high and healthy all along that distance. History shows that storms are inevitable.

Global warming only adds to this risk. Storm tides occur more often than in the past and they reach higher levels on average as well. The islands in the bay have been shrinking in size; some small ones have disappeared altogether. As the Greenland ice cap melts, tides will get higher still and storms will cut larger slices out of the dunes. All of which makes preservation of the beach itself a vital and expensive challenge for the future.

NOTES

[1]"Kismet's Old Dominy House," *Fire Island Light*, 23 September 1989.

[2]*Brooklyn Union*, 29 July 1885.

[3]Robert G. Müller, *Long Island's Lighthouses Past and Present*, 291.

[4]Ibid., 290, 291.

[5]Ibid.

[6]Ralph Middleton Munroe, *The Commodore's Story*, 41.

[7]Captain Charles Suydam, "Fire Island's Changing Lines," *Long Island Forum*, April 1942, 73.

[8]Madeleine C. Johnson, *Fire Island 1650s–1980s*, 173.

[9]*Fire Island Light*, fall (1990) 8, 15.

[10]*South Side Signal*, 30 July 1870.

[11]Frank Gulden, "More Old Hotels," *Long Island Forum*, August 1950, 152.

[12]*South Side Signal*, 6 June 1903.

[13]Benjamin F. Thompson, *History of Long Island*, Volume 11, 536, 537.

[14]Harry W. Havemeyer, *Along the Great South Bay*, 29.

[15]*South Side Signal*, 8 August 1874.

[16]James W. Shepp and Daniel B. Shepp, *Shepp's New York City Illustrated*, 362.

[17]George L. Weeks, Jr., *Some of Town of Islip's Early History*, 130.

[18]*South Side Signal*, 25 May 1895.

[19]Benjamin P. Field, *Reminiscences of Babylon*, 49.

[20]*Brooklyn Eagle*, 9 July1877.

[21]Ibid.

[22]*South Side Signal*, 7 May 1870.

[23]*Commercial Advertiser*, 19 August 1878.

[24]Ibid. by Howard Duke.

[25]George L. Weeks, Jr., *Some of Town of Islip's Early History*, 131.

[26]*South Side Signal*, 7 May 1870.

[27]Carl A. Starace, "Fire Island's Surf Hotel," *Long Island Forum*, August 1970, 156.

[28]*Commercial Advertiser*, 19 August 1878.

[29]*New York Evening Express*, 1879.

[30]Ibid.

[31]*Brooklyn Eagle*, 20 July 1886.

[32]Ibid.

[33]*Commercial Advertiser*, 19 August 1878.

[34]Ibid.

[35]*Brooklyn Eagle*, 13 July 1917.

[36]*Commercial Advertiser*, 19 August 1878.

[37]Carl A. Starace, "Fire Island's Surf Hotel," *Long Island Forum*, September 1970, 189.

[38]*New York Evening Express*, August 1878.

[39]*South Side Signal*, 21 August 1875.

[40]*New York Times*, 16 August 1875.

[41]*South Side Signal*, 23 September 1876.

[42]*South Side Signal*, 23 August 1879.

[43]*South Side Signal*, 1 January 1881.

[44]*Commercial Advertiser*, 19 August 1878.

[45]*New York Evening Post*, 10 July 1873.

[46]*New York Times*, 11 September 1882.

[47]*South Side Signal*, 4 December 1880.

[48]Axel Madsen, *John Jacob Astor, America's First Multimillionaire*, 270.

[49]*New York Times,* 29 June 1870.

[50]Charles G. Backfish, "Melville on Fire Island," *Long Island Forum*, April 1965, 71.

[51]Theresa Lanigan-Schmidt, "Herman Melville on Fire Island," a letter dated 7 July, 1885, *Fire Island Tide*, 17 July 1994.

[52]Madeleine C. Johnson, *Fire Island 1650s–1980s*, 94.

[53]Ibid., 96.

[54]*Brooklyn Eagle*, 18 January 1878.

[55]*Brooklyn Eagle*, 7 July 1891.

[56]*South Side Signal*, 25 May 1895.

[57]*Harper's Weekly*, 24 September 1892, 934.

[58]*New York Herald*, 19 September 1892.

[59]*South Side Signal*, 17 September 1892.

[60]Ibid.

[61]Edwin G. Burrows and Mike Wallace, *Gotham*, 1187.

[62]*New York Times*, 18 June 1894.

[63]*The Village of Babylon 1976 Centennial* brochure, 59.

[64]*South Side Signal*, 25 May 1895.

[65]Benjamin P. Field, *Reminiscences of Babylon*, 47, 50.

[66]*Brooklyn Eagle*, 13 July 1917.

[67]*South Side Signal*, March 1904.

[68]Captain Charles Suydam, "Changing Lines," *Long Island Forum*, April 1942, 73.

[69]"Queer Old Island Place," unknown newspaper, 29 July 1905, Long Island Collection or Queensborough Library.

[70]*Brooklyn Eagle*, 17 July 1882.

[71]*South Side Signal*, 6 April 1889.

[72]Ibid., 29 June 1889.

[73]"Queer Old Island Place," unknown newspaper, 29 July 1905, Long Island Collection or Queensborough Library.

158 ■ *Fire Island's Surf Hotel*

[74]*Harper's New Monthly Magazine*, July 1880.

[75]Benjamin P. Field, *Babylon Reminiscences*, 47, 50.

[76]Ronald G. Pisano, "The Tile Club and the Aesthetic Movement in America," 26.

[77]Ibid.

[78]*South Side Signal*, 27 August 1887.

[79]Captain Charles Suydam, "Looking Back at Babylon," *Long Island Forum*, January 1942, 8.

[80]Ralph D. Howell, Jr., *Alabama*, 4.

[81]Ibid.

[82]*South Side Signal*, 5 July 1876.

[83]Ed Meade, "The Story of Oak Island Beach," *Long Island Forum*, March and April 1983, 72–73.

[84]Captain Charles Suydam, "Looking Back at Babylon," *Long Island Forum*, January 1942, 8.

[85]Ed Meade, "The Story of Oak Island Beach," *Long Island Forum*, March and April 1983, 73.

[86]Ibid.

[87]Ibid.

[88]Ibid.

[89]Ibid.

[90]*South Side Signal*, 25 July 1876.

[91]*South Side Signal*, 16 September 1879.

[92]*South Side Signal*, 7 July 1880.

[93]*Brooklyn Eagle,* 18 January 1878.

[94]*Brooklyn Eagle,* 18 July 1886.

[95]*Brooklyn Eagle*, 22 August 1893.

[96]*South Side Signal*, 9 August 1902.

[97]*New York Times*, 28 May 1903.

[98]*New York Herald*, 29 May 1903.

[99]Ibid.

[100]*New York Times*, 3 July 1903.

[101]*South Side Signal,* 3 March 1894.

[102]Madeleine C. Johnson, *Fire Island 1650s–1980s,* 102.

[103]*South Side Signal,* 5 May 1894.

[104]Madeleine C. Johnson, *Fire Island 1650s–1980s,* 106.

[105]*New York Times,* 30 July 1894.

[106]*South Side Signal,* 19 January 1901.

[107]Henry R. Bang, *The West Fire Island Story,* 7.

[108]Ibid.

[109]Madeleine C. Johnson, *Fire Island 1650s–1980s,* 181, 182.

BIBLIOGRAPHY

Allen, David Yehling. *Long Island Maps and Their Makers: Five Centuries of Cartographic History*. Mattituck, NY: Amereon House, 1997.

Brandt, Clare. *An American Aristocracy—The Livingstons*. New York: Doubleday & Co., 1986.

Burrows, Edwin G. and Wallace, Mike. *Gotham*. New York: Oxford University Press, 1999.

Caro, Robert A. *The Power Broker*. New York: Alfred A. Knopf, 1974.

Field, Benjamin P. *Reminiscences of Babylon*. Babylon, NY. Babylon Publishing Company, 1911.

Havemeyer, Harry W. *Along the Great South Bay*. Mattituck, Long Island: Amereon Ltd., 1996.

Johnson, Madeleine C. *Fire Island 1650s–1980s*. New Jersey: Shoreland Press, 1983.

King, Dr. George S. *Doctor on a Bicycle*. New York: Rinehart & Co., 1958.

Madsen, Axel. *John Jacob Astor, America's First Multimillionaire*. New York: John Wiley & Sons, 2001.

Manley, Seon. *Long Island Discovery*. Garden City, NY: Doubleday & Co., 1966.

Mooney, Edwin J. *Ferries to Fire Island 1856 to 2003*. North Babylon, NY: C.E.M. Inc., 2004.

Müller, Robert G. *Long Island's Lighthouses Past and Present*. Interlaken, NY: Heart of Lakes Publishing Co., 2004.

Munroe, Ralph Middleton and Gilpin, Vincent. "The Commodore's Story," Historical Association of Southern Florida, 1966. Reprinted from the original 1930 edition.

Pulling, Sr., Anne Frances. "Babylon By the Sea," *Images of America*, Arcadia Publishing Co., 1999.

Thompson, Benjamin F. *History of Long Island, Volume II.* New York: Robert H. Dodd, 1918.

Weeks, Jr., George L. *Some of Town of Islip's Early History.* Bay Shore, NY: Consolidated Press, 1955.

Weeks, Jr., George L. *Isle of Shells.* Islip, NY: Buys Brothers, 1965.

ATLASES AND MAPS

United States Coast and Geodetic Survey, Southern Coast of Long Island-Western Part. Published in 1851.
Suffolk County: Map of 1858, 4 sheets.
Atlas of Long Island, New York, Frederick W. Beers & Co., 1873.
Atlas of Babylon, Bay Shore and Islip, Wendelken & Co., 1888.
Map of Long Island, Hyde & Co., 1896.
Atlas of Long Island, F.W. Beers & Co., 1902.
Atlas of Suffolk County, E. Belcher Hyde, 1902.
Map of Long Island, Hyde & Co., 1906.
Atlas of Suffolk County, E. Belcher Hyde, 1915.

DIARIES, ARTICLES, PAMPHLETS

Dominy, Felix. 1835 to 1846 unpublished diaries.
Hone, Philip. *Diaries of Philip Hone 1828–1851.* New York: Dodd, Mead & Co., 1889.
Bang, Henry R. "The West Fire Island Story," unpublished c. 1980s.

Bang, Henry R. "The Story of the Fire Island Light," 3rd Ed., Fire Island Lighthouse Preservation Society 1988.

Goggins, Francis V. "The Great South Beach Before 1910— The Tangier Smiths," an extract dated c. 1930.

Howell, Jr., Ralph D. "Alabama: A Vacation Refuge on Oak Island, 1896–2001," unpublished, 2001.

Lanigan-Schmidt, Theresa. "Herman Melville on Fire Island," a letter dated 7 July 1885, Fire Island Tide, 17 July 1994.

Pisano, Ronald G. *The Tile Club and the Aesthetic Movement in America.* New York: Henry N. Abrams Inc., 1999.

Village of Babylon—the 1976 Centennial pamphlet.

Shepp, James W. and Shepp, Daniel B. *Shepp's New York City Illustrated.* Chicago: Globe Bible Publishing Co., 1894.

Long Island Forum—several articles, see notes, formerly published by the Friends of Long Island Heritage, Inc.

NEWSPAPERS

Babylon Leader
Brooklyn Eagle
Brooklyn Times
Brooklyn Union
Commercial Advertiser
Fire Island Light (Published by Fire Island Lighthouse Preservation Society, Inc.)
Fire Island Tide
Harper's Weekly
Home Journal
New York Evening Express
New York Evening Post
New York Herald
New York Times
New York World
Newsday
Saturday Evening Review
South Side Signal
Suffolk County News

INDEX